ON TOP OF AFRICA

Neville Shulman OBE has had a very varied background in many areas of the Arts and is Director of the British International Theatre Institute, Vice-President of the Drama Centre, Vice-President of the National Children's Home Action for Children, Fellow of the Royal Geographical Society and Member of the Explorers Club. He has written for television and film, and has been a consultant on a number of documentary and short films.

On Top of Africa

The Climbing of Kilimanjaro

and Mt Kenya

Neville Shulman

ELEMENT
Shaftesbury, Dorset ● Rockport, Massachusetts
Brisbane, Queensland

© Neville Shulman 1995

First published in Great Britain in 1995 by
Element Books Ltd
Shaftesbury, Dorset

Published in the USA in 1995 by
Element, Inc.
42 Broadway, Rockport, MA 01966

Published in Australia in 1995 by
Element Books Ltd
for Jacaranda Wiley Ltd
33 Park Road, Milton, Brisbane, 4064

Cover illustration The Image Bank, Pete Turner
Cover design by Max Fairbrother
Design by Roger Lightfoot
Typeset by ROM-Data Corporation Limited, Falmouth, Cornwall
Printed and bound in Great Britain by
Redwood Books Ltd, Trowbridge, Wilts
British Library Cataloguing in Publication
data available

Library of Congress Cataloging in Publication
data available

ISBN 1-85230-617-3

Contents

'Above all the heights there is only silence.'

Goethe, 1749–1832

On Top of Africa is dedicated to all those who strive for the high roads, yet remember to care for those who stay below and can only stare at the heights, to Lela Hamilton, and to the memory of Willie Dunnachie who climbed Kilimanjaro with me but lost his way on another mountain.

Foreword

This is an inspiring book which says much about the total personal commitment needed to undertake any arduous expedition. Whether trekking through burning deserts and jungles or, as in this case, climbing two great African mountains back to back, this book emphasises the positive mental approach necessary when setting out to reach your ultimate goal.

The intense emotions that Neville Shulman experienced on this expedition are vividly described. His determination to allow nothing to deter him is admirable. Despite a host of obstacles, he eventually succeeds in his ambition to 'climb his mountains and know their summits.'

We all need a philosophy to see us through our darkest moments, and the one that Neville Shulman expresses so vividly in this book will undoubtedly help many readers face theirs.

Neville Shulman's climbs raised a considerable sum for a major children's charity and that undoubtedly added to his resolve, even when the way ahead seemed particularly bleak and the temptation great to give up. He attacks his mountains spiritually as well as physically, starting with the preparation phase. The spirituality of his philosophy should encourage us to reach our own personal summits and help us to guide others to climb theirs. It is immaterial whether the mountains are natural or merely self-created as we journey along life's unpredictable pathways.

Sir Ranulph Fiennes

How you hauled yourself up on that last day – the last of five such days – on the Machame Route, that endless last 4,000 feet on one good leg is still a source of wonder to me. It hurt just to watch and listen. I was tired on two legs. No wonder your doctors find it hard to credit, no wonder they cried impossible before and cried again impossible, after. On the soberest reflection, it is hard to believe – and I was there.

John Barry
(Leader Kilimanjaro/Kenya Expedition 1991/92)

'There is no height, no depth that the spirit of man, guided by a higher spirit, cannot attain.' Motives for climbing mountains, or surmounting any challenging and difficult undertaking are diverse. By no means all man's hopes and ambitions can be equated with selfless ideals. Yet I am sure that there is within us all an inner spirit, which can find its fulfilment through the challenges presented by nature.

I first met Neville Shulman at a reception for the Dalai Lama, one of the truly inspired human beings in today's much troubled world. Neville impressed me with his sincerity and his devotion to the theme of mountains in his personal quest for a meaning to life on earth.

John Hunt
(Leader 1953 Everest Expedition)

Preface

Although at first it might seem a contradiction, there is a direct relationship between meditation and action. Whether practised as part of the intense *zazen* of the Zen philosophy, or through any other form of meditation, the practitioner is concentrating the mental forces within, just as the mountaineer will additionally try to concentrate those physical energies needed to reach a particular goal and eventually the summit.

Any conflict that takes place within or outside the mind or body is a struggle with oneself, always seeking the spirit (*shin*) that governs the way forward. We are all a part of life, part of the universe, and what we do affects what happens to others as well as to ourselves. This relationship and responsibility is sometimes described as *karma*; a person's *karma* determines the next step along the way. Everything that has life also has *karma* and changes the way for those with whom there is some form of contact. A mountain is a living force and those that attempt to climb it should be conscious of its *karma*; its moods and strengths are volatile and it will react to and against those that venture there.

In our pressured lives we very often ignore or underestimate the value and importance of silence and solitude. It is less and less easy to find a silent corner to inhabit and to enjoy. There seem to be increasing intrusions into the way we are permitted to live, and this means that it is more important than ever to seek ways of insulating our being and strengthening our inner energies, so we can wander freely and more purposely along the paths we choose to follow.

There are few places on earth where an individual can

escape in order to re-think and understand experience peacefully and privately. A mountain is one such place. There a mountaineer becomes a philosopher while the physical strain of the climb provides opportunity for freedom and personal expression that will open the mind. But a mountain is also a humbling place; an individual will quickly accept the lesser role and realise how the mountain dictates the way to follow: 'To obtain enlightenment [*satori*] to any degree it is necessary to dismantle the ego.'

Injuring myself before the mountain expedition that is described in this book was a direct result, at a specific moment, of the lack of concentration I was giving to the mental and physical preparations needed. This injury added another dimension to the trip and meant that I would have to try that much harder. In a strange way that granted me a bonus, as it concentrated my mind and determination wonderfully, and caused me to try that much harder to accomplish the goals we had set ourselves.

One of the many reasons I have written this book is to encourage mountaineers, philosophers and all those who try, or need, to undertake some intense mental or physical activity. I hope they will find something within. To express it in the maxim often quoted, there is no gain without pain and I think the pain (*dukkha*) I carried with me on the mountains contributed to the achievements that we accomplished. Throughout the book I have included some of the philosophy, *koans* and information that helped me attempt and complete the expedition. Hopefully I have been able to express the benefits I derived from carrying my zen in my backpack along with my water and food. It is always important to remember that the mind also needs to eat and drink.

1

Why Two Mountains?

I have breathed deeply of the spirit of the mountains and want, perhaps need, to climb again. Even though my last, and first, mountain (Mont Blanc) has clearly revealed my lack of experience and technique, it has proved that the *shin* spirit that lies within each individual, if properly harnessed, can prevail against tremendous odds. Once more it should and could help me to tackle the challenges of another great mountain. Given the right mental and physical approach to the mysterious ways of the mountain, it should again be possible for me to meet and overcome its potent dangers. The philosophy and enigma expressed in the following simple poetic statement encourages me in my decision to go forward: 'He leaned his back on the cold rocks, his face shining like a full moon, although those on earth saw but one side.'

Of course this time I will not be so ignorant of how great the dangers can be. No amount of reading climbing books, looking at mountain photographs, even watching films of other climbers, can ever prepare an individual for the shock of attempting to climb a mountain, being there and feeling its magnificent forces bearing down on you. Your footsteps on the mountain are of no moment to the mountain itself, yet within the flickering light of human concern your attempt can illustrate the realities of death and survival, the conflict between the relative and the absolute. On the mountain you are always confronted by a statement of being and a seemingly opposing statement of nothing. The elements that exist on a mountain, constantly changing and transforming, cannot ever be fully described; they need to be experienced at first hand. They will etch themselves deeply into your memory, and thereafter your mind will always be able to recall the terrifying powers they possess.

Yet I also need another reason, perhaps a justification, that will underpin my will and determination to climb again. As always there is a *koan* that shows the way: 'Sometimes it is necessary to concentrate on the inner self, other times to alleviate social injustices.' My last climb had been generously sponsored to benefit children's charities. I decide that this next climb will benefit children's charities as well. But will it attract sponsors and donors as easily? The economic times have worsened considerably, and perhaps those who gave before will not want to, or be able to, support another mountain climb. I puzzle about this for some time, trying to think of whether and how this second mountain climb might attract sponsorship.

Suddenly the mists lift and the way ahead becomes clear. What is better than sponsoring one mountain climb? Why, sponsoring a climb of two mountains. It seems so obvious an answer that I am momentarily overwhelmed. But which two mountains, and how? Will I not be taking on too much, and how can such an expedition be organised?

I take down from my bookshelves a very old atlas and look through its pages, reading through the names of those faraway countries with impressive mountains and mountain ranges. There are not too many that contain two high mountains close enough to be able to climb both of them within a short period of time, particularly with names that are likely to be known and therefore attract sponsorship reasonably easily. Many people erroneously think of Mont Blanc as the highest mountain in Europe, whereas that honour in fact falls to Mt Elbrus in Russia (although in the past, as part of the USSR, it has often been considered as belonging more to Asia than Europe); Mont Blanc, more famous than Mt Elbrus, is merely the highest in western Europe. I need a mountain, and preferably two mountains, equally as well known.

Initially therefore I turn to those countries that have within their borders some of the greatest and highest mountains in the world – Nepal, India, China, Tibet. I am particularly drawn towards the fabled Mount Kailas of Tibet, revered by Hindus, Buddhists, Jains and all those who acknowledge the worth of ancient Tibetan culture and customs. Kailas (crystal) has many names and images; it is also called Meru or Tisé in its metaphysical form, as well as Kang Rinpoche (the jewel of snows), from which also springs the word *kangri*, snowpeak. *Ri* is the Tibetan word meaning peak; in its Zen context, however, *ri* also translates as inspiration, as well as representing the principles of the universe on which total truth stands. I therefore conclude that Kailas is in truth a mountain for another time, to be climbed for another reason, in isolation rather than in partnership. And on a practical level, I know I do not have sufficient time to participate in a climbing expedition to that area of the world, and indeed probably need more experience on the mountains before doing so.

I then turn to the pages on Africa and instantly, perhaps instinctively, know which two I should next attempt – Mt Kilimanjaro and Mt Kenya. One of my favourite writers has always been Ernest Hemingway. Writers, like artists and musicians, live on long after their deaths, some, perhaps like mountains, for ever, and are always referred to in the present tense. Hemingway is one of the great writers, whose works are cherished by succeeding generations and yet who was personally tormented by his own inability to cope with the mountains that life presented him with. One of his books, *The Snows of Kilimanjaro*, is an outstanding classic and within its magical pages it conjures up some of the spiritual and mystical qualities that are contained within and surround every mountain. Mt Kilimanjaro is certainly one of the most beautiful and awe-inspiring of all the great mountains, rising from its huge African plateau to tower magnificently 19,340 feet over its glorious surroundings. It is the highest mountain in Africa and its majestic presence commands the eye for hundreds of miles in all directions. It is now situated in Tanzania (still shown in my old atlas as Tangynykia), although it used to belong to Kenya. Queen Victoria, in those far off days when Kenya was part of the British Empire, gave Mt Kilimanjaro as a birthday present to her cousin, Kaiser Wilhelm of Germany, when Tangynykia was part of the German Empire; such was the prerogative of queens and kings in those colonial days that are fortunately no more. But for that royal gift, Kenya would have the two highest mountains in Africa, but now has to content itself with the second highest, Mt Kenya, at 17,038 feet.

The logistics of climbing Mt Kilimanjaro and Mt Kenya, back to back, are certainly possible, with a maximum of 14 days for the two climbs as an acceptable further condition to the challenge. I telephone John Barry, the very experienced team leader of my previous Mont Blanc climb; he responds enthusiastically and magnificently to the idea, and agrees to lead a team and make the necessary arrangements. He appoints David Halton to act as expedition organiser, and together they see that the timing and planning arrangements evolve smoothly. Subsequently it is decided that altogether there will be eight of us leaving from England, with two others joining us in Tanzania.

The commitment has been made. Now I must prepare myself.

2

The Two Highest African Mountains

Mt Kilimanjaro

Mt Kilimanjaro, with its glorious gleaming glaciers and its often wreathing veils of clouds, is an awesome and colossal mountain. Standing solidly and majestically amidst vast open plains, it seems to beckon you closer, inviting you to experience directly its magnificence. It is the highest mountain in Africa, 5,895 metres (19,340 ft) above sea level, and one of the world's highest free-standing peaks. In 1977 it was designated a national park by the Tanzanian government. It is part of the Great Rift Valley, called by many the cradle of civilisation, the birthplace of man. Kilimanjaro was first known to be ascended in 1889 by the German mountaineer Hans Meyer.

It is composed of three extinct volcanoes: Kibo, at 5,895 metres (19,340 ft); Mawenzi, 5,149 metres (16,896 ft); and Shira, 3,962 metres (13,000 ft). The highest point on Kibo mountain is Uhuru Peak (*uhuru* meaning 'freedom'). Gillman's Point is a subsidiary on Kibo's rim, at 5,685 metres (18,651 ft). Kibo, as the highest peak, is generally called by the all-encompassing name of Kilimanjaro, and has even been accepted as such by those who protect it and guide its visitors. The whole range is now a designated national park.

Kilimanjaro is located 330 km (200 miles) south of the equator, on the northern boundary of Tanzania. It rises from an open plain close to the Indian ocean, and its gigantic size and height strongly influence its climate and consequently its vegetation, animal life and, of course, its ever-changing climbing conditions. You ascend through farms, forests and giant heathers, then cross moors and highland desert, until finally you arrive at the eternal snows of Kilimanjaro – *kilimanjaro* means 'shining mountain'. During your ascent you can expect to experience equatorial to arctic conditions. The range begins with the warm dry plains, with an average temperature of 30° C, ascends through a wide belt of wet tropical forest, through zones with generally decreasing temperature and rainfall, to the summit where there is permanent ice and below-freezing conditions. For most months of the year there are few rainy days. The short heavy rainy season is usually from March to June, with some further monsoon periods in October and November.

Kilimanjaro has five major altitude/climate zones: the lower slopes; forest; heather and moorland; highland desert; and the summit. The zones occupy belts of approximately 1,000 metres (3,281 ft) each, and within each zone there is an association between altitude, rainfall, temperature, plants and animals. In general the temperature falls about 1° C for every 200-metre (656-ft) increase in altitude. Rainfall also decreases steadily with altitude, from the forest upward. Plant life is usually abundant in areas of high temperature and high rainfall, and decreases the higher you ascend, not because of the height but because conditions are much colder and drier. As animal life is also dependant on plants and vegetation, fewer animals live at the higher altitudes.

The lower slopes at 800–1,800 metres (2,624–5,906 ft) were originally scrub, bush and lowland, but this has been partly cultivated and is now used for livestock grazing and local crops. In this cultivated zone you are unlikely to see any large wild animals.

A band of extremely beautiful montane forest encircles the whole of Kilimanjaro at 1,800–2,800 metres (5,906–9,187 ft). This is the richest zone on the mountain. Because of the dampness of the forest and the altitude there is frequently a wide bank of cloud around this zone. Protected from the sun by clouds, the moisture cannot easily evaporate, so there is often high humidity, dampness and fog. Although flowers are not plentiful in the forest, those seen are very striking. The forest is also the home of most of Kilimanjaro's wild animals, although they are usually hidden from view. However it is possible to see both blue monkeys and the black and white colobus monkeys that live in the trees. A few leopards live throughout the forest, preying on antelopes, monkeys and rodents, duikers and bushbuck.

The heather and moorland at 2,800–4,000 metres (9,187–12,124 ft) is a sub-alpine zone with a cool clear climate, except for some mist and fog near the forest. Heather and heath-like shrubs grow in this area, as well as prickly gorse-like bushes, attractive grasses and flowers. There are not many large mammals here, and those that do visit the moorland are usually in transit to other areas, although elands, duikers, dogs, buffalo and elephants have been seen in this area. It is possible to see two types of buzzard, the Anguar buzzard and the mountain buzzard, as well as the crowned eagle and lammergeyer and the white-necked raven.

The highland desert at 4,000–5,000 metres (13,124–16,405 ft) is the real alpine zone. Here there is intense sunlight, high evaporation and huge daily fluctuations in temperature, falling below 0° C at night while in the daytime rising to as high as 40° C in the direct sunlight. Under these harsh conditions only the hardiest lichens, mosses and tussock grasses can exist. This area does not offer much in the way of wildlife, but its views are spectacular.

The summit lies above 5,000 metres (16,415 ft). This area is characterised by arctic conditions – freezing cold at night and often subject to a burning sun during the day. Oxygen content is about half that existing at sea level and the little atmosphere there is provides scant protection from the sun's radiation. Creatures of any size are rare in the summit zone, although a stray leopard was once found frozen in the snow.

Mt Kenya

The local name for Mt Kenya is *Kere Nyaga*, *nyaga* or *ngai* being the Masai word for God, also used by the Kamba and Kikuyu tribes. Mt Kenya itself is a twin-peaked volcanic spike, its main summits being: Batian, at 5,199 metres (17,058 ft); Nelion, 5,188 metres (17,022 ft); and Point Lenana, 4,985 metres (16,355 ft). The main two summits are separated by a col, the Gate of Mists, and can only be reached by using roped climbing techniques. The first known ascent of Batian was by Halford McKinder and his team in 1889, while Nelion was not conquered until Shipton climbed it in 1929.

Mt Kenya is located within the Mt Kenya National Park, 175 km (110 miles) to the north of the capital city, Nairobi. The great pedestal on which the Kenyan peaks are based has an approximate radius of 20 miles, although any ascent to the summits covers a far greater distance, due to the necessity to zigzag when climbing up and down the numerous ridges.

A trek on Mt Kenya traverses several distinct eco-zones. First there is the forest zone; here can sometimes be found elephant, buffalo and lion. The forest is also the home of the rare tree hyrax. Higher up is the bamboo forest, populated by several varieties of monkey. Next comes the moorland zone, which hosts a rich bird life including several species of birds of prey. Finally there is the alpine meadow, and the curious rock hyrax; 'rockies' are the nearest living relatives to the elephant, mainly through having the same long pregnancy-gestation period.

The flora found on the mountain can also be very rich. Due to the special geo-climatic conditions on Mt Kenya, many species of lobelia and groundsel grow to enormous dimensions; these plants encourage a rich bird and insect population, while their size often gives a weird visual effect to the landscape. There is also a profusion of exotic and unusual flowers. In previous years it was possible to see a number of wild animals around Mt Kenya, but it seems that these have gradually reduced, probably being caught and eaten for food.

Travel on the mountain during the long rains from mid-March to late June, and during the short rains from mid-October to late December, is not generally advisable. There are always serious dangers on the mountain and also on the tracks leading to the peaks. For this reason unaccompanied persons are not permitted to enter the park gates except for a day trip terminating no later than 4.00 pm. For a longer tour on the mountain the regulations require that a party consists of at least two persons, one of whom should be a guide or a porter. Permits and passes have to be checked when entering any park gate, and similarly on leaving the mountain area. Entry fees are payable. If you are overdue at the police station or a park gate, investigations start 36 hours after the time you said you would sign out.

3

Karma

It is possible to discover yourself on a mountain, any mountain, as if you have always been a part of that mountain, just as you are a part of those mountains that you will meet and climb while pursuing your own path in life. And all our mountains, no matter what their colour, size or intricacy, will need to be descended as well. A dream will not only become, but is the reality.

Our lives, indeed the world, unfold according to natural laws of cause and effect. *Dharma* (sometimes spelled *dhamma*) translates to mean law or the law of nature. When *dharma* is expressed we are following the law of nature, of which cause and effect are an integral part. *Karma* is explained as the forces, the conditions, the states, that shape a person's destiny. There is fixed *karma*, which should be unchangeable; for example, being born a man or a woman. Then there is variable *karma*, capable of change, over which we can exert some control; for example, conditions of health and states of mind.

An individual is always able to create good or bad *karma*, or even allow it to become or remain neutral and therefore of no consequence to the future. Our *karma* takes place initially within the mind; the thoughts formed are then followed by speech, which in turn is

followed by action. Our mental formations, called
sankhara, give rise to our *karma*.

We have new thoughts, new feelings, and create new
actions every moment. To these thoughts, feelings and
actions we attach the *karma* created in the past, and this
in turn is then carried forward to the future, our future.
We are all aware how easily anger and hatred continue
to live on in our minds, even seeming to feed upon
themselves; how fear and terror will not leave us; how
kindness and love stay with us; and we must choose
and decide which of these we will, and want to, carry
forward. If we felt anger a moment ago, we are not easily
going to feel relaxed and calm immediately. In contrast,
if we were loving, thoughtful and kind a moment ago
we should be able to continue those feelings. So we live
each moment with the results of the *karma* previously
accomplished.

We can all achieve a better *karma* for ourselves by
practising some form of meditation and trying to expel
those thoughts or emotions that are harmful or counter-
productive. Meditation regenerates the mind. Its aim is
to achieve insight into oneself, at a level that cannot be
attained by information or instruction. If a person is
fortunate enough to reach the ultimate depth of insight,
then that is known as achieving *satori* or enlightenment.
Satori is not necessarily a constant state; once gained, it
can be lost, and thus requires continued renewal. Additionally, meditation helps to combat unhappiness, or
at least enables it to be part of the whole, preventing it
from becoming destructive by balancing it with positive
thought and consideration. It is essential to accept
things as they are and not to long for them to be changed;
learning to accept the real world and trying to understand it is one of the important steps along the path to
satori.

Karma exists within all living objects or natural phe-
nomena. They have a need to exist. They are always

changing, although outwardly expressing permanence. A tree may stand for centuries, but each season it changes shape, height, loses branches and leaves and grows new ones. A mountain changes with the seasons: its rocks break and fall; the ice and snow melts or freezes; it may grow in height or diminish. The changes may be slight but they occur. Permanence and impermanence exist together and within each other, the one in the many, expressed infinitely in nature and within the constant rebirth in all things.

Karma causes or equals the birth and rebirth of our consciousness. Indeed, many would argue that each person's *karma* is all-encompassing; it touches every part of our being and the world we inhabit, and leads directly to the way ahead. If we continue to create bad *karma* for ourselves, and for those around us, we cause damage to our own spirituality, as well as to others, and we will be more likely to continue down a wrong path; we will then need far greater karmic strength to find the way back and to be able to follow again the right path.

'In a mirror you will not see your eyes, or anyone's eyes, only their reflection.'

4

Preparations

We know it will have to be a fast-moving journey of ascents and descents. We need to allow sufficient time to reach Kilimanjaro, attempt the climb to its summit, descend to our base camp, travel out and fly across to Kenya. There we will attempt the summit of Mt Kenya, make our descent and return to Tanzania in order to catch the agreed flight back to England. At one stage there is some talk of extending the length of the expedition to three weeks, but I need to be back in London earlier and also it is considered that the strict timetable will act as an additional spur to our efforts and make the expedition's success, assuming that to be the outcome, even sweeter.

Although Kilimanjaro is not really a very dangerous climb, it is going to be particularly arduous climbing its great height in a relatively short time. Furthermore, it might prove difficult to acclimatise in the five days we have allocated to reach its summit. It is also decided we will not use the usual and easier tourist routes, but climb up the Machame route, which is difficult and testing, although it should also provide better scenic views as a compensation. Two days will then be allowed for us to descend, with one travelling day to reach Nairobi, then three or four days to cover the trek up Mt

Kenya and our attempt on its summit. This will become at the final stage – the last 450 metres (1,500 ft) – a difficult technical climb, requiring use of ropes, crampons and ice-axes. We will have to take all this equipment with us, although initially can leave most of it at our base camp, to be collected after the return from Kilimanjaro. We will be able to use porters to carry the equipment on the lower slopes of Mt Kenya, but for the final day we will have to carry everything we need ourselves.

After the summit attempt it will take us one or two further days to get down and back to Nairobi, in order to take a flight back to Dar-es-Salaam on the next day and there to catch the connecting flight to England. There is little or no room for any delays, weather problems, mishaps or accidents – a tight schedule but just manageable. Barry and Halton continually emphasise the rigour and inflexibility of the schedule, and how each team member needs to be extremely fit and strong. They send through a programme of exercises to be followed in order to reach the peak of fitness they think necessary, or at least preferable. It makes somewhat depressing reading, as it doesn't really seem to allow for those of us who need to work right up to the date of departure, and who have a number of extra personal commitments to carry out. Still, I am determined to do what I can, and follow my own somewhat modified exercise schedule based on their suggestions.

I know that to balance my lack of mountaineering experience and expertise I will have to rely on the Zen meditative processes I practise. Although I can't prevent the fear of what I will be attempting from flooding into my thoughts, at least the Zen philosophy will allow me to deal with the fear, either to use it or to drive it away. In fact throughout the climbing this fear returns many times, and each time I try to use concentrated *zazen* to banish it again. Zen and the practice of meditation can help a person face up to any anxieties, whether from the past, the present or related to those that might take place in the future.

The Samurai warriors from the ninth century onwards invariably used Zen in their own mental and spiritual preparations for battle; they were trained and taught by the Zen masters of the day. Anything that would increase their chances of survival was adopted as part of their mental armoury. *Samurai* actually means 'those who serve', and originally they were chosen to act as defenders and bodyguards to protect the rich landowners from the marauding bandits. Often outnumbered, their psychological preparation allowed them to withstand surprise and otherwise overwhelming attacks. They developed their own traditions (*ryu*), becoming the greatest fighting force in Japan, known for their ability to overcome the greatest odds.

In my own daily training, continued on the mountain, I sometimes adopt the guise of one of these ancient warriors and try to conjure up imaginary 'demons' that I have to defeat. This make-believe game helps me to achieve limits of endurance and perseverance which otherwise would possibly have been beyond my capabilities. At times, when everything is crying out for me to stop and rest, I attack just one more 'demon' and so continue to run, to exercise, to train a few minutes longer. I carry with me in my training, and use again and again on the mountains, the inspiring words of instruction given to mediaeval samurai: 'You must concentrate and consecrate yourself wholly to each day, as though a fire were raging in your hair.'

Most of my running is carried out late at night, and this usually allows me to think through my mental preparations and condition my mind to accomplish the goals I have set myself. I am feeling confident and am impatient for the day of departure to arrive. I am perhaps too confident; perhaps my impatience unsettles my mental and body rhythms. One night, a night not to be forgotten, I am in a somewhat agitated state and this lack of calmness causes me subsequently to pay a heavy penalty.

Fitness and Training

There is no better way to become really fit for any serious physical activity, especially mountaineering, than to be generally fit already. Anyone who contemplates carrying out some major physical activity every so often should ensure that throughout their lives they remain in condition, exercise regularly and can therefore cope more easily when a greater physical stress is placed on their body. This should also be followed on a mental basis; you should prepare your mind by regular meditation, concentration and regular and active use of the mental faculties – reading, board games, even watching stimulating television and films.

As you build up to a certain activity or event it is important to increase your physical and mental training to reach a peak of fitness. In my case I evolve and try to continue a four-week training programme of jogging, running, running with breaks for exercises en route, press-ups, sit-ups, swimming or cycling and fast walking carrying a pack. The length of time or distance devoted to each activity is extended over the weeks, and the weight of the pack increased. One day a week is usually free.

Of equal importance, various specific exercises are followed to strengthen the ligaments and muscles of the legs, particularly around the knees and ankles. These include step-ups on to a bench or step; hopping on the flat, progressing to hopping up stairs; and using ankle weights while raising each foot. I think all mountaineers would confirm that it is in your knees, more than anywhere else, where you are likely to be vulnerable to problems, which can in turn cause your chances of success to be vastly reduced. I know from previous experience how important strong knees are in coping with the stresses of mountaineering and trekking.

Equipment

Any list of clothing for the sort of expedition we are planning must include not only boots (preferably well worn-in) but also trekking shoes. Because we will be encountering extremes of temperature, climate and terrain, we need both lightweight clothing as well as heavy-duty outer and inner garments. In order to allow us to leave certain items not needed on the whole trip at various places on the expedition, I am advised to include plenty of plastic bags and other coverings.

The equipment includes both a large rucksack and a smaller back-pack, a tent and a bivouac bag, as well as cooking and eating utensils, and practical items such as a compass, a head-torch and a hand-torch. Because we will be climbing, I also carry items such as ropes, loops, crampons, ice axes, and a harness with attached karabiners.

A comprehensive first aid kit includes antibiotics, aspirin, throat medicines, lip salve, eye-drops, a moxa stick, anti-diarrhoea tablets, water purifying tablets, malaria tablets, bandages and gauze.

I plan to carry a few books which will not weigh much but which will be useful to refer to and read at various times on the mountain, particularly when trapped through bad weather in a tent. I always carry a notebook to record my thoughts and the day's events.

Health

Unfortunately most areas of the world where it is still possible to carry out adventurous pursuits and activities can also be hazardous. For example when visiting East Africa various immunisations are necessary, including typhoid, cholera, yellow fever, meningitis and hepatitis. Malaria is now of great and increasing concern and required special consideration.

Although most of the time the expedition will be on the mountains, where the malarial mosquito is not found, we will have to pass through the lowlands, where it is. The advised course of malarial tablets is therefore essential – two tablets weekly (probably Nivaquine) and two tablets daily (probably Paludrine). The greatest chore proves to be starting the tablets two weeks before the journey and continuing four weeks after the return. The latter is essential. People come back from a journey to a malarial area, feel perfectly well and then assume there is no need to continue taking the tablets. Unfortunately many subsequently go down with malaria through neglecting their prescribed tablets. It is also necessary to be aware that in East Africa, and in fact in many parts of the world, there are new strains of mosquito that are proving immune to the present drugs, and therefore every possible precaution and medical advice should be taken and followed.

The sun's rays can be particularly dangerous at an altitude of 4,000 metres (13,000 ft) and beyond; at this level only about 60 per cent of the harmful UV rays are filtered out by the atmosphere. (Obviously, with the continuing depletion of the ozone layer this can now happen at a lower level and to a greater extent.) Skin can be rapidly burned and lips are often badly affected. We take with us good sunblocks, and wear dark glasses with proper side-panels to guard against snow blindness. (If snow blindness occurs it is essential to protect the eyes and to avoid rubbing them, if necessary band-aging them.)

The air at high altitudes becomes thinner, and the transfer of oxygen from the air to the blood is reduced. With less oxygen the body needs to work much harder to take in more oxygen, which causes a vicious circle whereby the body loses further necessary oxygen. Symptoms can include headaches, nausea, vomiting, diarrhoea, memory lapse, anxiety and insecurity, short-age of breath, and in extreme cases pulmonary cerebral oedemas causing brain damage and death. There are various tablets that can help to combat high altitude sickness, one particularly recommended for use being Diamox.

Infection, particularly gut infections, are always a great danger when it is not easy or possible to wash yourself or to clean the cooking and eating utensils properly. We always use water tablets to purify water for drinking and try to use boiled water or at least fresh water for cleaning. We look upon it as essential to dig a hole well away from the camp and pathways, in which we bury all our refuse, excrement and other natural matter and organic material. Our rubbish and other harmful items such as tins, plastics and bottles we carry away from the mountain. The mountain must be left as you find it and you owe a responsibility to those coming after you to protect it. As the Inuit saying goes, 'We do not inherit the Earth from our ancestors but borrow it from our children.'

5

Accident and Decision

My heart is already in Africa. I can sense the vast continent's heartbeats. In my imaginings I can already feel its heat and smell the scents of the bush plants and flowers.

My legs however are still very much in London, and I should show them more attention and keep my feet more firmly on the ground. But I am too impatient to be there, to finish with my preparations, the nightly training and running, to start the climb, and to touch the mountain itself.

My impatience must be passing itself downwards, unbalancing the inner calm that I know has to be so much part of my mountain attempt. My right foot twists savagely and I fall heavily, with all my weight bearing down without mercy as my leg crumples underneath it. Within seconds I am changed from being fit and strong and eager to someone whose right knee is wracked with pain. I hobble home and quickly ice my knee in a vain attempt to lessen the swelling, but I know that what has occurred is no minor wrench or twist of the knee joint, that it is considerably more serious.

If only I can claim back those vital few seconds and undo that moment. That thought continues to haunt me on the mountain nights as my knee throbs and denies me any rest. There is no doubt that many people's lives are changed dramatically, often tragically, by some event that occurs within a few seconds. If all of us were given the special gift, the power, the chance, to relive and change those few seconds in our lives, there is no knowing what we would gain as we undid the consequences of our actions. But that is not to be. I know I have to do what I can urgently to heal the injury.

I still have the telephone number of a physiotherapist, Sally Geater, whom I had used some years ago after a skiing accident. I telephone her, and quickly explain what has happened. She is fully booked up tomorrow, but is persuaded by my urgency and very kindly agrees to see me at 7.45 am before her other patients. I gratefully accept her offer. I spend a restless night, the first of many to come, as I constantly feel and touch my knee, vainly hoping that somehow the swelling has diminished and the pain has miraculously ceased. Unhappily that doesn't occur.

I am awake very early anyhow, so it is easy to get up in time and organise a car to take me to the address in London's Harley Street. I am there in good time and wait on the doorstep for the physiotherapist's arrival. She works in a clinic that initially has been created to look after the injuries and needs of dancers and choreographers, and this emphasis is noted in its rather odd title, the Remedial Dance Clinic. Its reputation has long ensured that sportsmen and sportswomen, amongst many others, make use of its excellent services. As soon as she examines my knee I can tell from the expression on her face that the news is as bad as I have been expecting.

'There's no way you can continue with your climbing expedition. You can hardly walk, let alone climb. You've ruptured the knee and certainly torn the ligaments on both sides, and at the very least it will take five or six weeks to recover. With less than 14 days to go before your trip means that it is impossible.'

I am shattered by the news and argue against her prognosis. She willingly agrees to my request for a further opinion, but of course her colleague, Shirley Hancock, confirms what she has said. I still don't want to accept their decision, so they agree to bring in their consultant doctor to examine my knee and give his expert opinion. In the meantime I am sent for X-rays so they can see if anything has been actually broken.

The subsequent examination by the specialist confirms that my knee is in bad shape and needs weeks of rest, and that I shouldn't climb. I argue with him that I have to continue with the expedition if there is any chance whatsoever, particularly as my climbs are being sponsored to raise funds for charity. I also explain the fact that the other climbers in the team have given up their winter holidays in order to join me. Seeing how much it means to me, the doctor reluctantly agrees to send me for a further stress X-ray, which will determine if my knee can stand up to greater strains than he thinks it can. I jump – metaphorically – at this remote chance, and hobble around to the nearby X-ray consulting rooms.

A stress X-ray is taken when one person pushes the top part of the knee one way and pulls the bottom part the other way. The X-ray thus records how much give there is in the knee and how much support remains. I steel myself to hold my leg as firm as possible, and refuse to scream as the nurse uses her considerable strength to manipulate my leg in both directions. She is surprised that it doesn't seem to hurt too much, and I ask her to make certain the doctor is aware of this. After some further physiotherapy, the doctor re-examines me, but still concludes that it is impossible for me to climb, advising that I should postpone or abandon the expedition. I explain that this decision is not acceptable, that it is still essential I continue, and ask if there is some way of supporting the knee, to allow me at least to make the journey and attempt to trek up the lower parts of the mountain.

After some further consideration he agrees to recommend me to a medical company in north London that specialises in knee-braces for sportsmen, to see what they can suggest. At first they offer me a heavy total-leg brace that fits outside my trousers and holds my leg firmly from the thigh downwards to the calf muscles. This is obviously impracticable. I explain that I will be climbing up and over rock faces, sleeping on the mountain at night in a tent. I need something that is less weighty and cumbersome, more flexible and that can fit underneath my trousers. The owner of the company finally produces a small stretch brace that fits around the knee. This will help in holding the bones and ligaments in place above and below the knee, while moveable steel rods provide side support. In the circumstances it seems the answer. I even start to feel optimistic. Zen insists upon self-reliance and now more than ever my own resolve will be put to that test.

I continue with the physiotherapy every two days, but the swelling refuses to vanish, although it does reduce. This means that I can't do any training, running or exercises, and even I finally begin to question the sensibility of going ahead with the expedition. After a week of treatment I feel I have to tell the other climbers what has happened, in case it affects their wish to proceed or to allow me to climb with them. Possibly I am hoping they will tell me that I am not being remotely sensible and that I must withdraw. I telephone the leader of the expedition and tell him I have damaged my right leg, torn the ligaments in the knee and it is still very swollen. 'Don't worry, you've got another one, you'll make it', is his nonchalant response. It is very much a mountaineer's response to injury, so very Zen-like, and again reinforces the strong correlation that I have come to realise exists between mountaineering and the Zen philosophy. I know now I have to proceed.

During the remaining few days I spend many hours trying to prepare my mental state, to come to terms with the additional immense physical strains that lie ahead. I have to calm my fears, and ready myself for whatever I might encounter on the mountains. My friends and colleagues do everything they can to dissuade me, but eventually they realise my mind is made up, that I am determined to go ahead. I explain that I doubt I will be able to complete the first climb and make the summit, but at least I can enter into the spirit of the expedition, make a token attempt and climb a certain distance up Kilimanjaro. What might actually happen I won't know until I am there and have started the ascent.

My physiotherapist continues to express her grave doubts; she thinks that at some stage my knee and leg will give up on the mountain and that then I might become a liability to the other climbers. I am very worried by this, but feel that I will climb at my own pace; if necessary the others can go on ahead and I will stop and descend if my strength and resolve weaken.

Strangely, throughout this period of pain and treatment, I start to experience a greater sense of calm and detachment than I have known before. Why has this occurred? Am I now more fatalistic about my prospects of success, or is it because I now have a justification in case of failure? In most great religions and philosophies pain and suffering play major roles, their leaders and prophets often undergoing supreme tests of courage, pain, torment and even torture.

The word *dukkha*, amongst many others, is used to express this suffering, and is one of the noble truths on the way to enlightenment. *Dukkha* need not necessarily be a physical pain; in fact it is rare that mental pain does not automatically follow on from a physical injury. It is always possible for any change, any activity, movement to give rise to *dukkha*. It continues always and exists within and is unlikely to disappear. If it does it will return. It is said that *dukkha* stands at the apex of transcendental experience, particularly when it is known the suffering will not be going away. This is a time when faith and confidence in one's self is vitally important, in order to live with the *dukkha* that is inherent in all aspects of our existence. It gives us the opportunity to look for something outside our worldly nature to offset the *dukkha* within.

Some time before the date of departure, a friend mentions that acupuncture has been known to help heal a ruptured leg more quickly than regular medicine. He wonders whether I should try this form of treatment, although it seems to me rather too late to do this now. Four days before I am due to leave I find myself talking with someone else who knows a herbalist who also specialises in acupuncture, and I then decide it is worth making contact with him.

I telephone Alan Treharne and explain the problem to him. He thinks that acupuncture will help, and that he can fit in two sessions, one tomorrow and one two days later. This is the first time I have ever undergone any acupuncture but I am willing to undergo any treatment that might improve my chances. After arriving at his home I lie down on his couch and he examines my swollen knee and decides the particular acupuncture points into which he will insert the needles. He opens a new packet of needles, chooses three and painlessly inserts them. He also fixes pieces of a herbal substance called moxa to the tops of each of the needles and sets the moxa alight, explaining that the fumes from the moxa encourage the knee to heal itself more quickly. The burning of the moxa and the acupuncture treatment last about 20 minutes. He then gives me a moxa stick to take with me, telling me to burn this twice a day, allowing the fumes to flow around my knee.

During the following two days I use the moxa stick as he has directed, and hope that it will have the desired healing effect. I can't really tell if it is working as the knee still looks and feels very swollen. I have my last treatment of physiotherapy. Sally Geater and her colleagues wish me every luck on the expedition although still feel that what I am doing is incomprehensible and very unwise. I try to banish their doubts from my mind. I need every particle of mental strength to help me overcome the lack of physical strength in my knee, as well as cope with my reduced fitness due to the lack of training over the last two weeks. I visit Alan Treharne for a final session of acupuncture, and at his clinic at least receive some mental encouragement and support for my actions. He gives me another moxa stick to take with me to the mountains, advising me to use it whenever I can, to burn it regularly and allow the fumes to heal the knee.

During the few days before departure I have gone out for walks of about an hour, wearing the knee-brace. I want to make certain that I can actually walk whilst wearing it, and to try to work out what are the physical consequences of using it. My leg feels very tired after one hour, and at that time it seems to me very unlikely that I will be able to finish the climbs. In fact I think I might only make it through the first day before my knee gives way under the strain being placed on it.

Some people have said that I don't have the ghost of a chance, but I know that many people, the Chinese particularly, believe that ghosts (thought of as guardian angels to some) often give encouragement to those who call upon them. I hope that perhaps in using the Chinese moxa stick I am calling upon the ghosts of my past, or of the mountains, and that they might help me continue along the way.

6

The Expedition Sets Off

We are to catch an evening flight from Gatwick airport, outside London. I am driven to London Victoria railway station, and from there catch a mainline train down to Gatwick. The train I take is meant to be an express, but some accident has occurred somewhere on the line and the train just crawls along. I don't mind too much as I am quite early, and it gives me more time to think and try to prepare myself for whatever might be ahead and whatever I will encounter, on the journey and on the mountains themselves.

Despite the train's delay, I am the second member of the team to arrive. The first is a very tall American, Jim McWilliams, experienced in mountaineering in the United States and bringing with him three huge canvas bags in which he has packed all kinds of climbing equipment, cameras, books, medical supplies and a multitude of clothes and other items. My one backpack looks insignificant and quite minor in comparison. The other team members then gradually arrive and we exchange names and greetings. Apart from John Barry, the leader of the expedition, I have not met any of them before.

We check in our luggage at the desk of Tanzanian Airways and try to find out from their staff our exact flight route. There are some differing opinions: one of them thinks that we can fly directly to Kilimanjaro airport at Sanya; others announce we will have to fly first to Dar-es-Salaam, then take a smaller plane on to Kilimanjaro. Either way we will certainly be flying via Rome airport, and it is therefore likely to be a long and tiring night. There is plenty of time to spare, so we wander off to purchase some books and to find something to eat. I don't remind John Barry, or tell anyone else, about my leg injury. It seems rather inappropriate at that moment, and I know they will find out soon enough.

The only food counter open is run by an inexperienced, rather young, man, with a very winning smile but who unfortunately suffers from immediate memory lapse. He finds it difficult to remember any order, and certainly the whole order; even when he has eventually organised the food, he then forgets who has ordered what. We spend some rather surreal moments trying to order food, pay for it and eventually obtain it, but it is a way to pass the time.

Eventually our flight is called and we board the plane. On board we find out that it first has to fly to Charles de Gaulle airport in Paris, then go on to Rome, then to Dar-es-Salaam, and finally to Kilimanjaro airport itself. However our luggage has only been booked to Dar-es-Salaam; there we will have to disembark, go through Tanzanian customs, then board a different aeroplane to take us on to Kilimanjaro.

Through most of the journey, by chance or otherwise, I sit next to one of the climbers, Ian Newell, who is a Buddhist, and this gives us an opportunity to discuss our interests in various forms of philosophy and the many ways of stimulating energy and gaining physical strength. In particular he recommends *t'ai chi*, the process of using slow physical movements to contain and concentrate one's energy. In performing *t'ai chi*, he explains, it is necessary to imagine one is holding balls of energy, which are slowly expanding, thereby creating tremendous strength. I tell him about my knee injury, and he advises me to concentrate on using all my mental forces to turn the knee pains away and to try to hasten the healing of the ruptured ligaments. His advice is sound, and through much of the flight I meditate and use the technique of *zazen* to free my mind and then to concentrate my inner forces. *Zazen*, although usually practised sitting in a traditional posture, can be practised in any position, even whilst walking. The essential point is to breath correctly. The attitude of mind generated in *zazen* is called *hishiryo*; it is a state of thought that occurs without thinking, seeking out the consciousness beyond thought.

Some time during the long flight we find out that our aeroplane first stops at the Kilimanjaro airport before going on to Dar-es-Salaam. As our luggage has been ticketed to Dar-es-Salaam, it could mean that we will not be able to claim it even if we get off at Kilimanjaro; the alternative is to continue on to Dar-es-Salaam and then catch another plane back to Kilimanjaro. It is at this time that I start to realise how Africa, particularly black Africa, abounds in, and almost relies on, enigmas and riddles. After some lengthy discussions we are able to re-organise the luggage arrangements, so that when we land at Kilimanjaro airport we can check through all the luggage and take off those pieces that are ours.

The Tanzanian customs arrangements turn out to be far from straightforward. We are initially asked for additional visas, which we are told should have been issued by the embassy in London. Fortunately, after production of a press card and some fervent arguing, the necessity for the extra visa is waived. Of course, as we have now landed at Kilimanjaro rather than Dar-es-Salaam, there is no one to meet us and it means we have to organise our own transport to take us the 20 km (14 miles) to Moshi, the small town from where most of the climbing expeditions commence. At Moshi we have been booked into the relaxing Mountain Inn for the first night, in preparation for an early start the next day.

We arrive in the late afternoon and are able to share some comfortable double rooms, all of which have internal showers. I wander out into the gardens so as to burn the moxa stick, and use it to heat and to help heal my knee. I am soon surrounded by a number of Tanzanian youngsters, who vie with each other to stand closest to the circling smoke. The smell from the fumes wafts everywhere, and brings everyone out to find out what is happening. I explain as best I can; no one really understands, but all are highly amused.

Afterwards I watch some giant lizards gently and slowly circling and chasing each other on the walls of the veranda, as if the sport is not really to catch each other but merely to provide entertainment for the onlookers. We go to bed early, and I cover myself in the mosquito net I have brought with me. There is no way of hooking it up to the ceiling, so it has to lay across me. During the night my head starts hurting, and eventually I realise I have blocked off most of the oxygen, so throw off the net and decide to risk the mosquitoes.

I can't sleep now, so listen to the soft and varied sounds of Africa. There are many false dawns, as the cocks decide to crow from 2.00 am onwards. At first light though, I hear one solitary bird, seemingly situated immediately outside my window. I listen to its beautiful, distinctive voice; it seems to be singing just to me. Eventually several others join in, and their chorus of voices fill the morning. When full daylight finally arrives the pulsing sounds of the cicadas are abruptly silenced, and the night totally vanishes. Before I get up I to try to channel some strength and energy into my knee, and place my hands on my stomach to use its *hara* force.

Today I hope to taste and feel the magic of Africa.

7

First Day on Kilimanjaro

The owner of the Mountain Inn, Mr Harshna Shah, arranges a full breakfast for us and at the table we meet the two other members who are joining our party. We now number ten. We leave behind in the hotel our passports, most of our money, various valuables and any other un-needed items. It has been explained that on the mountain, as you climb higher, particularly if you are suffering from altitude sickness, you may become vulnerable to the 'ghosts' that sometimes take what they can from unsuspecting travellers. I am to learn that in Africa there are many kinds of ghosts.

In this region monsoons usually occur twice a year and the ecosystem depends on them totally. We are told that the November and December monsoons haven't yet taken place and are very late. This is very worrying, for several reasons. During at least half the year most of the land is dust covered and almost totally barren; when the monsoon rains occur, sometimes lasting for days or even weeks, these barren areas can spring forth lush grass carpets, which in turn will then attract and nourish the huge herds of wildebeests that roam the Serengeti, the Ngoron Goro and Arusha parks and conservation areas, above which can be seen Mt Kilimanjaro, dominating with its massive presence. (It's really only when you see the mountain from a great distance, or more particularly from an aeroplane, that you realise its immense size). We are further told that either the monsoons would not now occur, in which case the droughts would continue with devastating results for wildebeest and the Tanzanians; or else the monsoons would come suddenly and might even overtake us during our climb. Selfishly we hope the monsoons will hold off for a week longer, but if there has to be a choice there is no doubt whose need is the greater, and so we join in the silent prayers of the Tanzanians, waiting patiently as always for the rains to come.

We make our final preparations and discuss possible routes, but all agree we will not trek up the Marangu route, the usual tourist route and certainly the easiest way of reaching Uhuru peak. Uhuru is the highest point on Kibo, which in turn is the highest peak of the mountain. It seems strange that Hans Meyer only reached the summit just over 100 years ago, but perhaps it has something to do with the way that, for all time, mountains have been treated as holy, magical and special places where most people are frightened to intrude.

We board two jeeps and are driven through the town of Moshi to the travel office. There we arrange to pay for our park fees and the porter hire. Our jeeps are then driven to Machame village where there is a wide green surrounded by huts. Our African porters are waiting for us to sort out their individual loads and decide what food, cooking pots and other items we will need. They then will carry them for us up the mountain. It is extremely hot, and we strip down to T-shirts and shorts and prepare our own smaller backpacks in which to carry water, some extra clothing, cameras and a few other items we might need between now and the time we reach the Machame Hut.

I strap on my knee-brace and everyone gathers around, to examine both the brace and my knee. People become more fully aware of the damage the knee has suffered and can see how swollen it still is. It feels very strange to be starting off on Kilimanjaro in this way, with such a handicap, and I hear the excited chatter of the African porters as they watch me closely. I imagine that they are trying to understand what has happened to my knee and why I still want to climb, and possibly are wondering how long I will continue before I have to give up. I try to comfort myself with one Zen understanding of many, seemingly impossible, truths: 'Consider a metal ship floating on water.'

The Machame green is set at about 1,500 metres (4,900 ft), so we still have 4,400 metres (14,500 ft) to go to the summit. It is a very daunting prospect, but I try to put any gloomy thoughts away and feel and enjoy the warmth of the day. The beauty of the surroundings lift my spirits and I hope this will help carry my legs a greater distance. We start off along a very easy path that winds its way slowly upwards, mostly through cultivated areas. Our team are soon strung out, with me towards the back. The porters, despite their heavier loads, are way ahead. A number of the climbers have hurried on, but I am anxious to pace myself and to test out my knee more slowly.

There are various support systems used to maintain rhythm and energy when carrying out any physical activity. Invariably these involve breathing steadily and consciously. For now I content myself with counting my breaths in and out. I count 'One' on the in-breath and a further 'One' on the out-breath, then 'Two' on the next in-breath and 'Two' on the next out-breath. This is continued up to ten counts each, then I start again. If my mind wanders and I forget which number I'm on then I start again from the beginning. It helps me to continue without too much difficulty and I feel pleased at my initial progress.

We reach the park gate, where everyone has to regis-

ter. The signing-in book is not very full, as this is
obviously a route that is not often used. We are now at
Nkweseko and have perhaps been walking for about
one hour. The gatekeeper leaves us to make our own
entries and we feel excited and even light-headed. In
some way this feels more the start of the adventure and
our climb. But only half of us have written in our names
and registered when the heavens suddenly open and
there is a heavy downpour. There is nowhere else to
shelter so we all crowd into the park hut and wait for
the rain to abate. It continues for perhaps half an hour,
then gradually lessens and, wearing our rainproofs and
over-jackets, we again set off following the track that is
to take us upwards to the Machame Hut.

Initially we walk through plantation and vegetation,
which is relatively easy to handle. The others are now
far ahead of me. Gradually the climb becomes tougher
and my knee is really hurting. I turn the pain away and
allow it partly to remain behind with each step. I
remember that within our physical bodies of pure flesh
there is concealed an unrankable being who often
leaves and enters through the doors of our faces. We are
composed of so many parts and players.

It continues to rain, only slightly, but enough to make
the ground soft and slippery. Then the tropical downpour returns with a vengeance and soon I am completely
soaked through. Even worse, the earth underneath becomes extremely unstable, so that every time I place a
foot on the ground it invariably slips, causing tremendous pressure on my knee as I strive to hold myself
steady. There is nothing for it but to continue onwards
and upwards. I have to climb along numerous rocky
pathways and scramble over twisted and gnarled tree
roots as we head on into the forest. It takes me some
further five hours before I reach the Machame Huts, of
which there are three.

All the other climbers are huddled inside one of the

huts, and all are as soaked as I am. The porters have lit
a fire inside the hut to try and help us warm up and dry
out, but because the wood that has been used is damp
there is a great deal of smoke from the fire, and it is
extremely painful to the eyes. I crouch down as low as
possible to try and avoid the smoke. In that hunched
position I change my clothes into somewhat drier ones,
although I find that my pack has been soaked through
by the rains and the clothes in it are also damp. I
gratefully drink the tea that is offered and, unusually,
put in a lot of sugar, hoping that it will provide me with
more energy to continue.

Dinner is prepared by the porters, but it takes many
hours to organise and it is not until 10.00 pm before it
is completed and brought over. Meanwhile we have set
up all the tents. I carry my large pack and my smaller
backpack into my shared tent to try and sort myself out.
My sleeping bag is too wet, so I crawl inside the bivi
bag with all my clothes on, and try to make myself
warm. Gradually it becomes very cold and I find I
cannot sleep. I spend most of the night lying there,
listening, trying to energise my leg and reduce the pain.
The words of Zen Master Setcho spring to my mind:
'Words reach from edge to edge.' Will my thoughts
similarly reach out to the mountain and lift me some of
the way? I must never forget the simple truth: 'A mountain is a mountain, a stream is a stream.' There is still
some light rain, but at least no major downpour occurs.

I get up very early next morning in order to spread
my wet clothes amongst the trees and bushes in an effort
to dry them. This is not successful as there is little wind
and insufficient time. I decide what I should wear on
the next part of the climb, what things to take with me
in my backpack and what to pack into the rucksack for
the porters to carry for me. I put clothes and other items
inside various plastic bags in an effort to keep them
separate and dry. The clothes I am wearing are both

dirty and damp, and it is certainly not a great way to continue. Another tropical downpour ensues, and I try to protect myself as best I can, although not very successfully. All I can do is try to think warm and dry thoughts and remain positive.

8

Three Days More

So far we have climbed to 3,000 metres (10,000 ft). Yesterday we climbed some 1,500 metres (5,000 ft) from the Machame village. Today's climb will be much shorter; our goal, the Shira Hut, is set at 3,840 metres (12,700 ft), but it will be a much tougher and, in parts, steeper climb.

I have constantly to stretch both my legs to reach the footholds, and the strain on both knees is immense. The knee-brace is a boon, but I must watch carefully how I plant my feet to limit the stresses caused. At first it is extremely hot and I wear a cap to shield me from the burning sun. We climb slowly through the thick vegetation. I am breathing hard as I will myself to keep moving forward. It is hard work but I know I mustn't stop if I am to maintain any kind of pace. The others are way ahead of me as usual, and they are able therefore to stop more regularly to rest. Eventually I catch up with them as they stop for a longer food and water break, grouped round a large rock set immediately above me. They seem to be watching my efforts with some amusement as I slowly scramble up to where they are. They appear so relaxed, and I nonchalantly wave away their friendly concern.

I wait with them for only a few moments before

deciding to go on and lead on the route ahead. I know they can catch up with me whenever they want to, but I must push on while I can. I pass the Lager Stream and the winding deep valley it has created. The team leaders soon reach me again. They decide to break for lunch, and we wait for all the others to join us. I can't tell whether they are tiring or just taking it easier. Anyhow, it gives me a few moments within which to meditate. In doing so I know I must try to transcend the conscious-ness of the struggle so far and the struggle ahead. Whatever I have gained is a gain. My mind eases, and I enjoy the wild African scenery.

I don't want to rest too long. I am determined to keep going, and after some 10 minutes decide to set off again and head up through the rocks. The path is relatively easy to follow, but it is hard and painful to my feet, and the hard pounding particularly affects my knees. I stop before an enormous rock, perhaps some 5 metres (15 ft) high, which blocks the way. Somehow it has to be scaled. I feel extremely nervous about the strain it will put on my knee, but have no choice but to attempt to climb it. I slowly work my way up it, my backpack all the time pulling me downwards, then cling to the rock face, hoping that my footholds will not give way and cause me to slip. I finally reach the top of the rock and with relief pull myself over it. I still refuse to rest. The route continues along various steep ridges and rocky paths that I have to work my way along painfully. It seems as if the path is zigzagging backwards and for-wards, meandering between and around the rocks. Sometimes I cannot easily locate the path, but it doesn't take very long before I find it again.

Three of us, Willie Dunnachie, Ian Newell and I, are now climbing together. We reach the shelter of a large overhanging rockface and decide to stop for a while. Immediately the rains start again – not too fiercely for us to go on, but I certainly don't want my dried-out clothes becoming wet again. Under the shelter of the rock I pull on over-trousers, over-jacket and my thin cotton balaclava and set off again. This path is much easier; there's hardly any gradient, and all I need to do is keep going at a steady pace. Along the path there are various markers to follow – sometimes an orange sign, sometimes a piece of wood pointing the direction. Often there are rock signs, a smaller rock placed on top of a larger rock, similar to the rock signs of Tibet.

We reach the Shira Plateau. To the west are rock formations called the Shira Needle and the Shira Cathedral. It is now mostly scrubland, with bushes sparsely spread across the very rough terrain. I can see some smoke rising ahead, and after crossing a small stream and rounding the side of a sharply edged rockface, I see that our porters have based themselves in a large deep cave. They have decided we should camp here rather than go on to the Shira Hut, which is a few hundred feet further onwards. They have lit two or three fires and are busily making tea, and I am very glad to stop and rest. I unload my backpack, slump down at the entrance to the cave and wait for the others. It is only mid-afternoon, but there is no sun visible and I sense that it is going to be a very cold night indeed. Sitting perfectly still I can feel the blood drumming heavily in my ears. It proves easy to open my mind, not to anything, simply to open my mind, unlock another door.

We pitch the tents and sort out our various bags and packs. I hope that the slight breeze will help to dry out our wet clothes, so I drape mine around some sparse bushes, which bend under the weight. One of the team is already feeling the effects of the altitude and is suffering with a headache. All he can do now is rest and hope it will not worsen.

Today we have climbed for some six hours, and I am somewhat surprised that my knee has stood up to such considerable stress. The knee-brace is a great help;

without it I doubt whether I would have been able to struggle up this far. In the downpours my moxa sticks had become wet and unusable, but now finally they have dried out. I find a place to light one of the sticks and allow the smoke to curl around my knee. I hope that it is helping. I know I have to think that it is. It is essential that I retain this positive attitude all the time if I'm to have a chance to make it through to the end, whatever that might be.

Next morning the decision is made by the guides that, instead of climbing much higher that day, we should head eastwards to the Barranco Hut, which is only 3,950 metres (13,000 ft), just 110 metres (360 ft) higher than the Shira Hut. It is felt that this will enable us to acclimatise more slowly and suffer fewer altitude problems, while at the same time we should experience some magnificent views of the Western Breach of Kibo. We should also have excellent opportunities for some spectacular photographs of the mountain and the glacier walls.

The idea sounds great in theory, but for me it turns out to be the most painful day so far. This part of the plateau is a series of ridges and valleys, which means that we are constantly ascending and descending, climbing up over a ridge, only to have to climb down into the next valley. Climbing downwards is often more of a strain on my knees than climbing upwards. Furthermore, the mists come right down and we all feel cold, wet and very tired. We have split into several small groups, and our particular guide seems to take us the longest way round. We cannot tell whether he is lost or not, as he always exudes extreme confidence. Invariably he underestimates the time needed to complete each section, and I find this frustrating. I don't know whether he does this in error or whether he feels that it would be more encouraging for me to think that there is only a little further to travel. He doesn't realise that for me only the truth will complement my mental approach.

We are also getting concerned about some of the others; it is very easy to get lost on the mountain, and we have heard stories of several climbers disappearing in the mists and never being found.

We have to cross several streams, including the two large ones, the Lager Stream again, and the Bastion Stream. It is heartbreaking work as we toil up a steep slope, only to be told that we have to descend the other side in order to make our way across the further ridges that cross our way. At times I think that we have traversed the same area twice, and become convinced that we have travelled in a circular fashion, increasing the distance we have had to cover, rather than taking a more direct route.

Altogether we continue trekking and climbing for some nine hours before we reach our destination, the Barranco Hut. I am in great pain and have strong fears that I will not be able to continue further. I am mostly silent as I try to think through the possibilities. My strained legs are becoming extremely weary, and I feel that my chances of success, of reaching the summit, are very slim. So far, though, I haven't had any real problems with the altitude, but I guess that is because I have had to concentrate so much on my knee, fighting to combat the pain.

I am quiet throughout that evening, and feel myself withdrawing more and more from those around me and from my surroundings, as I continue the battle within. In the tent I cannot sleep. My knee is throbbing and whichever way I turn or lie it hurts. Also my clothes are dank and dirty, and I feel cold, no matter what other clothes I put on. The rest of the team are just as weary, of course, but they don't have the disadvantage of a ruptured knee. There is nothing anyone can do to help; it is entirely up to me whether I go on or not. It is a very long night, and in the morning, having hardly slept, I am feeling very despondent.

If I am to continue I must strive to find a system of meditation and purpose that will provide me with the right view of the mountain. There is negative meditation and positive meditation. Negative meditation, preferably undertaken in the lotus position of crossed legs and cupped hands, allows one to move one's mind into deep internal meditation, with no conscious thought intruding. The mind vanishes from the present and enters a time zone all of its own, apart from reality, apart from life itself, never being the Now. Positive meditation, on the other hand, can be used to overcome pain, exhaustion, even fear itself. It can keep you going when everything is screaming at you to stop, to give up.

We are to continue our circular climb of Kibo, although today we will be climbing higher; the Barafu Hut, our next stop, is at 4,600 metres (15,000 ft). This also proves to be a very long wearisome day. We are in the high desert area, where it is very cold and damp, with plenty of mist at all times. At brief moments it is just possible to see to the right the great Barranco Huge Ravine dropping down in the distance. There is no sign of life. Our porters, wearing long waterproof coats, carry the heavy sacks of the food that we will need for our last night. There are certain water points that we have to reach each day in order to fill up our containers, and I realise that this governs the route that the chief guide is taking. My progress is slow, and I fall further behind. I now have to fight a constant battle against tiredness, pain and exhaustion. On the mountain everyone has to think primarily about himself or herself, and it would be unfair for me to expect otherwise. I know everyone is feeling the strain, and try not to express my own thoughts to my fellow climbers. They have their own battles to fight.

It takes us some seven hours before we reach the Barafu Hut. There we have the choice of sleeping in the hut or in our tents, but as I don't feel like sleeping anyhow I join most of the other climbers in the hut and lie down fully dressed. One or two are feeling very sick, and are unable to eat. I force myself to eat more than I want in order to boost my physical strength, and I cover my food with salt and have several cups of very sweet tea to ward off possible altitude difficulties. The head guide is very worried about my fitness and condition, but I assure him that I want to continue and will attempt the final climb the next morning. The ideal time to leave is early, at around 3.00 am.

This is obviously a much tougher expedition than any of the climbers had expected, possibly because of our choosing the Machame route. Certainly we have covered a greater distance than most climbers, and in a shorter time. The monsoons have also caused problems; indeed the weather conditions have really been against us throughout. Furthermore I am convinced that the guides have taken us on a longer route than was warranted, or perhaps have just lost their way several times. In the mists it is very easy to do just that. Just like in the mists of Life.

9

Attempting the First Summit

Whatever I have endured previously, I know that this is going to be by far the toughest day of all. We have to climb a total of 1,300 metres (4,300 ft) in one day to reach the peak, and if I make it then of course I must still climb back down to reach the Kibo Huts far below. We also have to carry extra water and any food we might need. At this high altitude the strain, mentally and physically, is absolutely immense. With my legs at times seemingly on fire, I am going to have to struggle with all my determination to continue the climb. I know that above all, in order to succeed, I have to understand and practise non-attachment. I will have to fight with all my might the delusions that will attempt to mock and divert me. I have learned that, if you can control it, pain can sometimes become your ally; this belief will be tested again and again throughout the climb. I still don't know whether I have a real chance of achieving the summit or whether I am going to have to give up at some time on the final ascent.

We are in the south-east valley, and from now on it is an extremely steep climb over hostile ice and rutted snow. It is excruciatingly cold and we have to put on whatever clothes we have with us, in an endeavour to protect ourselves from the freezing temperatures and the fierce biting winds. I know it is possible to meditate away the feeling of cold, although I don't know how it is possible to generate actual body heat. I have read about the Kargyuna monks who, in sub-freezing temperatures, had wet towels placed on their bare shoulders and were then able to raise their body heat to the point where the towels would dry out. This process is known as *thumo reskiang*. There is also a technique of raising your body temperature by massaging the pressure points in the flesh between the thumbs and the forefingers. I doubt whether I would be able to accomplish this, and hope that it will not be necessary.

The American climber with the team has loaned me one of his ski poles, and I am using this extensively to balance and to help prevent some jarring of my injured knee. It is of great assistance, although often my foot still slips, either from tiredness or because the ground is so uneven – probably both. When this happens a sharp pain shoots through my entire leg, and sometimes I can't hold back a cry of agony. My shout stops everyone in their tracks, and they watch to see whether I have had enough and will finally give up and go down. But the cry of pain erupts after the pain itself, and this gives me a moment to pull myself together, concentrate my mental forces, use the *dukkha* within, and I take that further step upwards.

We have split into two teams. The first team comprises six climbers and three guides, while I am in the slower second team of four climbers and two guides. The four of us are soon strung out as my progress gradually becomes even slower. The head guide has stayed with my group, and he continually urges me to give up and make my way down to the Horombo Hut, where we will stay the night and where the rest of the porters are waiting for us with our other equipment. I know he is thinking of my welfare, but I am abrupt and rather aggressive in my reactions to him. I am not prepared to give up, and I wave away any assistance he offers. I am determined I am going to do it in my own way or foolishly perish in the attempt. I know these thoughts to be somewhat melodramatic, but I put my behaviour down to the high altitude and the constant pain I am feeling. The second guide, Ambrose, decides to help me by leading me directly. He moves down to step one or two paces in front of me, so that I don't have to work out my route and can simply follow after him. It is a warm and generous offer, and proves to be a great help. The ice is almost rock hard and extremely slippery, but Ambrose forces his boots into the ice in order to give me the chance of a firmer foothold. He zigzags his way slowly upwards, and I follow behind him as closely as I can.

I understand that there are energy lines created by everyone, actively or passively, and which it is possible for others to tap into and use as an energy force. You often see this being played out in a race, when one runner will set out as a pacemaker for the other runners; they then follow behind, until at the right moment they are able to increase their speed and pass the lead runner. I have always felt that in some way they are linking into and using the pacemaker's energy and power, without using up so much of theirs. It seems like a good time to try this out. Mentally I try to attach myself to Ambrose and gradually link into his strength and rhythms, feel them becoming one with mine. Where he steps, I follow exactly. Almost hypnotically I force myself to match his speed and rhythm, and I steel myself to ignore the pain from my legs. It is as if I am joined to him, and I sense his surprise and the surprise of the head guide as I then continue to climb upwards, matching myself to his steady footsteps. I am becoming very hot and undo my outer coat and other clothes, even though at the very same time I can feel the intensity of the wind biting deeply through me. Everyone else is totally buttoned up, but there is so much heat coursing through me that I am sweating. Is it the energy I am creating or perhaps the energy I am drawing on? The final climb feels as if it is going on for ever, but I have no real conception of time. All I know is that, whatever happens, I will continue.

I feel myself connecting constantly with the four primary elements of earth, water, fire and air. Earth is the element of solidity, the hardness of the ground and ice beneath my feet. Water is the sweat, the saliva, the coursing of the blood through me, as well as the element that binds Ambrose to me. Fire is the temperature, not only the extreme cold, but also the energy I am creating. The air is all around me, the wind screeching its harsh messages to all that will listen, and the breath within my straining body. In Buddhism there is a symbol known as *mandala*; in Hinduism it is known as *yantra*. Both combine the circle (water) within the square (earth) containing two crossed lines, in all representing four paths or doors. A standard yogic exercise is to place oneself mentally within such an image, searching for a deepened sense of earth consciousness. You are always seeking natural harmony through a balance of opposing forces – between earth and water, male and female, light and dark, between yin and yang in Taoism, between yab and yum in Tibetan tantric tradition. These thoughts and images pass through my mind whilst it struggles constantly to force the body to continue.

Despite all my efforts I start slowing up, and Ambrose also slows. It feels as if we are part of a dream sequence, my moving in slow motion, with the reality only occasionally penetrating when I allow myself to become fully conscious of my legs and the constant pain they are experiencing. We are now a long way behind the first team, and I know the climbers in my team are becoming more and more concerned at our slow progress. Barry suggests I give up if I can't keep up the pace, but I refuse to accept that as a possibility. I brusquely tell him to go on and leave me behind as I will make it, no matter how long it takes me. At present there isn't a way to explain my thoughts and feelings to him, and perhaps when we return it may be too late or no longer necessary. There is a saying, which again tightly relates philosophy and mountaineering: 'When the mind gives up, the body ceases to function.'

The landscape is so bleak and it is so very misty. The wind is coursing around me with such a force that often I almost overbalance. At times I have to lean heavily on the ski pole to hold myself upright. I grit my teeth so as to try and prevent any sound escaping, but even so a few times I have no choice but to scream out and then wait until the knee pain subsides.

Many hours later, long after everyone has given up trying to dissuade me from continuing, we arrive at the very last steep icy incline. I hear a voice shout down to us from one of the first team who has waited behind. I guess it is some words of encouragement to me. Zen Master Kasan once stated: 'The many mountains abide in the one mountain, the many voices go to the sea and disappear.' I have indeed climbed many mountains this day, and the one voice I hear I know carries the voices of many.

I struggle up that last section for what seems like ages. It is a particularly bitter and exposed forsaken area. It is easy to talk to myself, and I mutter and try to remember some *koans* that relate to my situation. 'Now where is human nature? I only know I am in the middle of this mountain. But the clouds are so thick I cannot figure out where exactly I am.' All I can and must do is climb higher. 'A lonely pine flourishes on top of the winter mountain.' I don't expect to find one here on Kibo, but I will find something.

Eventually we reach Gillman's Point. This is the place that those going up the tourist route usually stop at. It is certainly an achievement in itself, but I haven't come this far, suffered so much, to stop here. The leader of the first team, David Halton, has waited for me whilst his other climbers have already started their descent. He leads me and the other three climbers towards Uhuru Peak, the two guides remaining behind. Halton tells me it is only a short distance away, but I know he is only saying that to encourage me to go on. It is not that steep or even painful, but the altitude makes it extremely tiring. Strangely and encouragingly, I notice that the other climbers seem to be feeling the altitude more than myself. After we pass the Wedge there is Elveda Point at 5,885 metres (19,420 ft). 'When the mountain has been climbed the landscape of the goal appears all at once.'

Uhuru means freedom, an apt name. I feel a great sense of freedom as I reach the Tanzanian flag that stands at the highest point of all Africa. I remember one of the classic Zen replies from the seventh century, simply stated by Master Hui-neng when asked whether it was a flag or the wind moving: 'Neither. It is your mind that moves.'

I know it is utterly cold, but somehow I cannot fully feel it, even though the wind roars its fury and power around me. Perhaps foolishly, I take off my hat and bare my head for a few moments in silence and thanks. Kibo is an extinct volcano, and to one side there is the gigantic ash pit from those ancient days when the volcano was vibrantly alive. I don't think a volcano ever dies, though; deep down there is always a force, a power, which can be reawakened. It is like a slumbering giant that only needs a special word, a moment, to make him shake his fists and terrify his world again. I stand where Hans Meyer had stood, and many others after him, and there are a few wonderful moments of peace when all the pain completely vanishes and I know that my struggle has been truly worthwhile.

10

Descending Kibo

I am very reluctant to leave the summit. I want to allow this glorious moment, these wonderful feelings, to last and last, but I know it is not possible. Hui-neng's words again seem somehow apposite. 'In what I have just revealed there is nothing hidden. If you look within yourself and find your true face, then the secret is in you.' I have already overstayed my welcome. Quite suddenly, finally, I become totally aware of the absolute bitterness of the wild wind that roars incessantly at this incredible height. The coldness is now taking over every part of my body, even my mind, and I quickly realise that the high altitude is also sapping my will. We will take just a few more photographs, then we must start to retreat.

As we descend, we pass to the left the huge Reusch Crater, and beyond it through the mists I occasionally glimpse the Eastern Ice Fields. Progress is steady as we clamber down through icy passageways and over rocky outfields that test my resolve as I try to place my feet in a straight line to avoid any unnecessary jarring. We reach Elveda Point again, trek past Hans Meyer Point, Stella Point, then Bismarck Tower, and continue on to Gillman's Point, where our two guides are waiting for us. We then gradually make our way down through the ice fields, 5,500 metres, 5,400 metres, 5,300 metres. The ice is vanishing and we are on to scree and gravel tracks, loose and slippery – ideal descent conditions for two strong feet, but for me it means there is no support, my legs slip and slide and I have to use the support of my arms and the ski pole to prevent myself toppling over on many occasions. The others race ahead and for most of the time vanish from sight.

I pass Hans Meyer Cave at 5,150 metres (17,000 ft), and begin a very painful and long haul over many rock outcrops as I follow the track down and make for the Kibo Huts. There is no problem now with altitude; all I have to contend with are the leg pains, which are now trying to dominate me. I long to rest, but realise it will only cause more delay and won't help me to recover. I continue at my own pace, though often slowing down so much that I feel frustrated by the small amount of ground I am able to cover. Eventually I reach an even track with a sign to Kibo and I know I am nearly there. Some stone cairns point the way. Every so often I pass some strangely built large mounds of stones, and subsequently learn that these are graves of those that have died previously on the mountain. Some of them remind me of the Chinese burial tombs formed into a semi-circle of stones to represent the womb of the mother.

As I limp into Kibo I am overcome by the welcome planned by the other climbers. They have formed two lines through which I am invited to enter so they can cheer me and toast our joint success. I am completely overwhelmed by their warmth, but at the same time am frightened to show my own feelings too much for fear I might loosen my determination, as I know that there is still a long way to go before the expedition ends. Although for the others it is now a relatively easy climb down the side of Kilimanjaro, through the Marangu forest, for me a great deal of torment and pain still lies ahead. I need to remain strong and determined throughout the descent.

The Kibo Huts, at 4,700 metres (15,500 ft), can house up to 120 climbers, but there is no natural water available and supplies have to be brought up from below. They are really only a sleeping place for those trying to climb up to the summit who need to rest and acclimatise. So after only some minutes we start on the long walk down to the Horombo Huts, where we are booked to spend the night. The Horombo Huts are 1,000 metres (3,300 ft) lower, so that it is still quite a distance to cover. We pass a number of tarns, beyond which I can see the rising distant glaciers leading to Mount Mawenzi, well beyond the Saddle and the local area known as the Camel's Back. We cross some wide dusty plains, called Triplets, littered with stones that have rolled down over the centuries, where the track is relatively easy to follow. We then pass Middle Red Hill, West Lava Hill and East Lava Hill. There are some wonderful, exciting rock formations, as well as small intricately shaped rocks, some of which I pick up and examine before placing back as rightfully belonging here. The route takes us in front of Zebra Rock, and after that we sight Horombo and reach the complex.

Like the Kibo Huts, the Horombo Huts are extensive, with some amazing facilities when compared to the starkness of the Barafu and Barranco huts we had used on our ascent. The latter had just been small tin huts, built only for shelter, without water or any other facilities, whereas Kibo and Horombo are built for the many that trek up the tourist routes and need to stay in large huts overnight whilst they acclimatise. The Horombo Huts can house up to 200 persons, and have cooking facilities, lavatories, outside water taps, and even sell beer and cola. They also have rats. At one stage I enter the kitchens to find one of our guides, and see several rats, obviously ignored or tolerated, gnawing quite contentedly at the huge sacks of rice. It becomes clear that lack of hygiene in these huts is also tolerated. In these circumstances it is essential to take extreme care in what and how you eat and drink, but when you are tired and exhausted it is not easy to be too careful. I presume many climbers just take their chances, and conclude that a proportion probably go down with dysentery and possibly a lot worse through failing to take precautions at the huts. It seems such a great pity that someone can spend so much effort and energy in climbing Kilimanjaro, only to be laid low by the lack of facilities on the descent. Whenever I order a drink I take it directly out of the bottle, refusing to use the glasses that are brought to us, as I guess they are just dipped in the ordinary water – the same water from which the rats drink. I am very hungry and need the food that is available in the dining hall, but eat only the hot cooked food, hoping that this will act as some kind of protection against the unhygienic conditions.

I take a walk outside whilst it is still light. I can see across to the Mawenzi mountain, which reaches to a height of 5,149 metres (16,992 ft). Not many people bother to attempt to climb it, but it still looks like a very interesting mountain and worth considering for the future. It is certainly a great sight to see these two noble mountains, Kibo and Mawenzi, on the horizon, magnificent, majestic and timeless. I lose myself in time and practise *zazen*, as far as it is possible in a standing position. It is always preferable to meditate in a *zendo* (a room used especially for meditation), but I prefer the outdoors *zendo*, in the shadow of the mountains, to the stifling crowded rooms full of impatient and uneasy bodies and minds. To obtain the deepest concentration it is necessary to develop harmony in the body and the mind. When entering a *zendo* the student (in one way we always remain a student) bows, whether others are present or not, places the palms of the hands together (this is called *gassho* in Japanese) and bows again to the cushion on which he will sit. This acknowledgment

Mt Kilimanjaro : the dream to achieve

Mt Kilimanjaro reveals its majestic immensity

The author with a guide on the lower ranges

The late monsoon arrives, requiring a change of outer clothing

Trekking up the lower snow slopes

Climbing high above the Shira Plateau, the air thinning rapidly

Standing on Kilimanjaro's summit, Uhuru Peak, with the
Tanzanian and NCH flags

Receiving his Kilimanjaro certificate-the author
and his guide Ambrose

The final aerial view of Kilimanjaro on the flight to Kenya

At the foot of Mt Kenya's three peaks, the magnificent
Ice Couloir clearly visible

The daunting ice routes
to the summit of Mount
Kenya, photographed
from base camp

Climbing up the rocks to
reach the assault camp

Ice-axing up the final tortuous 1,000 feet

represents the respect you always need to show to your true self. Then you finally bow to any other students present, to show them true respect. In *zazen* the Zen masters will tell you to sit with noble strength, like an iron mountain, so it seems proper and right in this place to stand and bow towards Kilimanjaro in respect and gratitude for allowing me to visit and return safely.

For the first time for five days and nights we are able to rest and sleep in beds. They aren't up to much, just narrow bunk-beds in long wooden cabins, but they still seem very inviting. The blankets are quite dank, have obviously been used many times over and are presumably hardly ever washed, perhaps once a season. I prefer the top bunk, as it seems less closed in, but it is painful to haul myself up in order to lie on it. As best I can, I hang some of my clothes from the rope lines in the hut, to try and air them and dry them out. There is no electricity, so everything has to be done before the light fades, or by torchlight. A number of those staying in the huts are on their way up the mountain and there is a lot of movement after it becomes dark, as people come and go, undressing noisily in the darkness, or sorting out equipment and their backpacks for the morning. I don't envy them, knowing what lies ahead.

Suddenly I start to feel sick, and think I am going to choke, finding it difficult to breathe through my throat. I struggle out of my bunk and painfully hit the floor as I misjudge the distance. With the aid of my torch I fumble in the darkness to find the aspirins. I decide to gargle with some water in order to clear my throat and to try and kill the infection that I feel must be building up. There is nowhere in the hut itself where I can do this, so I have to put on some clothes and my boots and, still using the torch, stumble down the dark staircase into the downstairs dining-room. I need to dissolve the aspirins before gargling with them, then realise that I didn't bring any cup with me. I can't face going up the narrow stairs and disturbing everyone again, so use a glass from the table, hoping that it will not cause me any infection. The gargling helps, and eventually I make my way hesitantly back up the stairs and clamber again into my bunk. I know I have disturbed most of those trying to sleep, but there is nothing else I could do. I pass an uncomfortable night, lying on one side so that my throat won't become choked again.

In the early morning I feel really bad. My face is probably as grey as the light around me. I have a hot breakfast, hoping that that will help, and we make our final preparations for the last long trek down the rest of Kilimanjaro. We are to exit by the main park gate, Marangu Gate, which means a descent of nearly 2,000 metres (6,600 ft) to the Park headquarters at some 1,800 metres (5,940 ft). The ground is still very wet underneath and it rains from time to time as we climb down. We pass through all kinds of different vegetation and terrain, following narrow forest-paths, scrambling over huge tree roots that are twisted and turned in every direction. These are particularly painful for me to climb over. Sometimes the earth gives way and I slide forward, trying to limit the strain on my knees, although knowing that the pain will occur and be there the moment I stop myself or am stopped by a tree-root. It is a long and arduous process.

We pass Podocarpus Hill and the Maundi Crater, and after many hours reach the Mandara Huts at 2,700 metres (8,900 ft). Normally the huts can sleep up to 180, and we were hoping to find drinks and other things to buy, but unfortunately the huts, although open, are not in use and there is nothing available. We rest for a while whilst I examine my knee and change the bandages and knee-brace to a different position to make it feel more secure. I meet a number of climbers on their way up, and most of them sympathise with me, assuming that I have hurt my knee somewhere on the mountain. It is too long a story to explain that I hurt my knee in England before the climb, and that I have managed to make it to the summit wearing the knee-brace; it would sound an impossible story to them, and it seems an improbable one to me now. Fortunately I have the companions and the photographs to prove it, not only to others but also to myself. In some ways the whole expedition seems like a dream. Perhaps that was partly why I was able to accomplish it.

We continue the long slow painful descent down the mountain and again I am soon far behind the other team members. I am not worried now, though, as I know the way ahead. The final descent involves climbing down through the forests, where there is a great deal of water; it has obviously rained even harder on these lower slopes than above. One sight will always remain in my memory. Along a fairly even and wide path I see my first lion. In fact it is a lion's head superbly carved out of a broken tree stump, framed by raffia strands to resemble his mane.

The last few hundred metres are well signposted, with relatively good tracks, the soft, wayside grasses feeling like feathers after the rocks and stones. Finally I find myself entering the well-ordered Marangu Park entrance. I am ushered through to an open cabin with tables and chairs, where park rangers insist I fill in a questionnaire about the facilities I have encountered and those I would like improved. I must look a strange sight – dirty, tired, unshaven, mostly unwashed, limping in with my knee-brace. The rangers are smartly dressed, and I can see the amusement in their eyes as I try to respond to their formal questions. The other climbers have been waiting patiently for me for some time, but now they hurry me up; they are anxious to return to the Mountain Inn at Moshi, some 15 km (10 miles) away, in order to clean up. There are trucks waiting for us, and we say an emotional and warm farewell to our guides and porters, who have helped us through so magnificently and been so much part of our achievement. We give them a few clothes as souvenirs, although I know I owe them so much more, particularly my guide Ambrose. I shake hands with all the guides and porters. 'Sisi ni raliki, the Swahili for We are friends.'

The shower I take at the Mountain Inn feels absolutely incredible, and I soak myself for a very long time to wash off the grime and dirt of all those days and nights on the mountain. Still feeling the pain in my throat and in my ears I start a course of antibiotic tablets, in case any infection has arisen, particularly from those very unsanitary conditions at the Horombo Huts. As always I am last out, and dinner has already started. The head guide and Ambrose have joined us, bringing the signed certificates to present to all of us to acknowledge that each one of the team has successfully climbed Mt Kilimanjaro to its highest summit, Uhuru Peak. We share some wonderful moments of comradeship, laugh together a great deal, all of us knowing Africa has opened its arms to us and we have exchanged heartbeats.

11

Moshi and Mackinder

The next morning we receive a 5.30 am wake-up call. We breakfast quickly, collect all our luggage together and board a coach to take us to Kilimanjaro Airport. There is some time to spare before flight departure, and I visit the airport shop. I do not want to add to the weight of my luggage but purchase a carved ebony walking-stick to provide some further support to my very tired right leg. The flight out takes off at 8.30 am. The pilot kindly circles Kilimanjaro and Kibo several times so that we can have one last look and take photographs. The mountain is so beautiful, superbly magnificent and quite wonderful to behold, and it silences me as the memories flood back. It seems impossible that some three days ago we actually climbed it and stood at that summit, but that is truly the reality.

The rest of the flight is peaceful and quite uneventful. I come across a copy of the Tanzania *Daily News* and read details of the tremendous floods that have taken place throughout the country during the last few days, arising from the late monsoons. It also reports on some cholera outbreaks, particularly in the countryside. At Nairobi Airport we are met by Andy Black of Natural Action, the travel company making the arrangements in Kenya. He helps us load all the luggage and gear into his jeep and then drives us on the route out to the Naro Moro River Lodge. On the way we stop at the Fig Tree Hotel to order a full English-style breakfast – eggs, sausages, bread and tea. After I finish I still feel hungry, and order a second round. The Fig Tree Hotel is rather an odd place as it seems to offer every kind of service and facility, including the use of sauna and massage rooms at the back of the hotel. I take the opportunity to burn some moxa to try and ease some of the knee pains.

The rest of the journey is long, and halfway to the Lodge we stop at an outside restaurant and shopping centre to order some refreshments. As we have been informed that things go astray very easily, we park directly in the centre's compound, next to where the drinks are served, so that we can keep an eye on the jeep and the luggage. One of the team decides to buy a safari hat. I decide I would also like one, but think that the price is too high and try to negotiate it down. However the voluptuous sales lady is not persuaded. After we have finished, and as the jeep starts to pull away, the price drops rapidly, but now I have decided not to buy.

We arrive at the Naro Moro River Lodge. Instead of staying in the Lodge buildings, as we had expected, which have comfortable rooms and showers and full facilities, we are to tent in the grounds. This is rather a disappointment as we were hoping for some luxury before setting off, but it has to be accepted. We sort out the available camping sites, put up our tents and hang out those clothes that still have to be dried out – most of them in fact. We then head into the Lodge for drinks and a well-earned dinner. After all it is Christmas Day. There is a special dinner available, as well as all kinds of entertainment. A local choir starts off singing gospel; this is followed by some energetic acrobats and then there is the break-dancing competition. My weary legs luckily prevent me from participating. We make the most of the civilised surroundings and enjoy an unusual evening.

The next day I get up initially at 7.00 am, but then decide to take it easy for a while longer in order to rest. I realise I am feeling exhausted, and my painful leg needs all the rest it can get. We enjoy a huge breakfast over at the Lower Lodge, and decide to leave some of our clothes and various items behind, including my new ebony walking-stick. We then pack ourselves into the jeep, which takes us up a series of winding roads until we arrive at the meteorological station. There we make camp, set up the tents and prepare for the next day's climb.

We have now been in Africa 10 days, although it feels so much longer. We wake up just before 7.00 am and prepare a mixed breakfast. The porters arrive shortly afterwards, load up and we all set off at around 8.30 am to trek to Mackinder's Camp. It is going to be a long exhausting hike up through the boggy and marshy areas. On leaving the met. station and passing by the radio station the track becomes a clear path and continues to climb through forest before suddenly breaking out into open heathland. On a clear day the entire Aberdare Range can be seen to the west, on the other side of the wide flat Nyeri valley. The first of the red and white marker posts is reached, indicating the route through the steep boggy section known as the Vertical Bog. If there has been a dry period this is not too difficult a section, but in wet seasons this can be extremely wearing and difficult. We are unlucky; it has rained extensively and we have to try and avoid the many wet holes that seek to suck our feet downwards. The gradient eases and then, on passing through the forest, we get our first view of the main peaks. The path gains height, keeping mainly to a small rock ridge. At one point the path passes below and to the right of a series of low cliffs, offering us some shelter from the wind and sometimes blocking out the rain. The path continues to climb, still following the marker posts, until a fork is reached at an advantage point overlooking the Teleki Valley. The left path drops steeply to the Naro Moro river, then follows the river upwards on its northern bank. The path to the right drops more gradually to cross the river at a point 3 km further upstream. After the paths have converged again the way continues towards the head of the valley, past the signposts indicating Mackinder's Camp.

The landscape around reflects the special happiness of this great country. Everything in the shining morning light seems young, fresh, clear and open after the constant showers of rain. Sunlight filters through the foliage and is broken into a thousand reflections on the streams of water that run softly over the smooth multicoloured stones. The beauty of the images astounds me. 'If we understand something rationally but do not love it, there can be no completeness, certainly no fulfilment of purpose. If we love something but do not understand it, the same also applies. It is necessary to love and understand at the same time.' The undergrowth is often so thick that only by carving out a trail with an axe or bush knife is it possible to pass through it. On the river bank there are flowers, some shining like dancing flames against dark backgrounds, others hanging pendulously towards the water. There are yellow swords of gladioli, bell-flowers, pale pink or ochre-striped orchids and thistles with monstrous purple heads. We come across carcases of old trees that have been struck by lightning, or have died of old age, sometimes spanning the pathway or the streams and showing their pitiful useless roots, often already covered by newer and stronger vegetation. I can hear the exhilarating sounds of some wonderful birds and occasionally am lucky enough to see some of them; graceful sunbirds with slender beaks and bright colours, harshly croaking lories showing in flight their blood-red wing feathers. Butterflies of all kinds dally gracefully along the river bank and dart amongst the trees.

As we ascend I try to help myself up by holding on to the roots of small trees or grasping protruding stems and heavy creepers. I soon realise what it means to disturb the old plants of the forest world; the roots I grab hold of transfer the motion through to their parent plants, which, quivering and shaking, in turn transmit it to other plants, tufted bushes, slender bamboos. A number of dead bamboos, which if never touched might have remained for years, more or less as they were, even though rotting, suddenly fall towards me. I have to dodge out of the way several times as thorny plants and heaps of dead leaves and twigs are dragged down in their paths.

I see some strange signs and writings on a number of the boulders that we pass on the way to the Camp. One of the porters tells me they were written by previous climbers as signs to aid those who had got lost on the mountain in the mists. Unfortunately sometimes the climbers vanish forever, and the signs then become their memorials.

Eventually we arrive at Mackinder's Camp at around 2.30 pm, where we see a number of rock hyrax. As soon as I've unloaded my packs I roll up my trousers, burn a moxa stick and use the fumes to try and ease the pains in my knee, hoping it will help it recover a little, but it remains painful and sore.

The afternoon is cold, bleak and very wet. I rest as much as possible, as there is little else to do except read and help prepare the food. At this altitude of 4,250 metres (around 14,000 ft) water has a much lower boiling point than it does at sea level; this means that it is necessary to boil water for much longer to be as effective as usual – not so important for making some drinks, certainly coffee, but for good tea it means a much longer wait. The more I can rest the better for my knee, so I try to keep warm and lie down in the tent. I find it impossible to warm up, and spend a very cold night indeed, perhaps the coldest night of the expedition so far. Everything is cold and icy, and probably as a consequence my knee feels frozen and even more painful. I use the moxa stick again to try and loosen the knee joints. I realise my right hand is also quite swollen, and burned from the strength of the overhead sun, although I hadn't realised this when it was happening. However, this is of little consequence in comparison with the pain in my knee.

I have carried my *dukkha* with me throughout my journey on the mountains, and now fully realise how heavy it has been. I cannot run or hide from it and must continue to use it as a strength rather than a weakness. I am too weary to feel and experience too much and try, succeeding occasionally, to practise *mushin*, the art of 'no mind'. I remember that there is no real difference between an ordinary person and an enlightened one, only that the ordinary person believes experience is concrete whereas an enlightened person is aware that life is both empty and concrete.

12

To the Gate of Mists

It is the final day. I wake up at first light. My knee is frozen and stiff and I dress slowly and clumsily. At this stage I can only hobble about, and it takes some time before my leg loosens sufficiently to allow me to walk. Edwin, the lead porter, and the other porters soon arrive from their camp, set a little distance from ours. They start collecting up our packs and gear to carry them for us to the next camp. We then load up our own small backpacks and start walking up the ridge towards the area known as the American Hut (although there isn't any hut there). As I climb and traverse the hillsides, I stumble through what appears to be a wonderful botanical garden: white helichrysum bushes; cushions of mosses and tiny flowers; all seeming to have been planted by hand, as if to show off to the world their gorgeous contrasts of colour and leaf. There seems to be every shade of yellow, pale and dark, ivory, and all kinds of greens, from the deepest to the brightest emerald. The air is cool and extraordinarily clear. Looking backwards I can see a series of hills, spreading out in the distance, clad with green and brown forests, then the yellowed barren plains and green-blue rivers stretching out in a seemingly limitless spectacle.

To catch my breath and summon up my strength, I

stop in the shade of a rock wall, quaintly and oddly
sculpted by the winds and the rains. At times it seems
as if a primaeval silence hangs over the rolling plateau.
The gentle slopes are covered with dark-green giant
heather, draped with the long grey lichen known as old
man's beard. The undergrowth is sometimes knee-high,
and often I have to force my way through it, using up
valuable energy and strength. There are a great number
of the white papery helichrysum flowers. The grasses
here do not form any kind of lawn-like carpet as is often
found in the Alps; instead they are coarse knee-high
tussocks and clumps, separated by foot-deep ditches
that have been created by the rains. Sometimes these are
so well hidden that I stumble into them, causing my
knee to give way, and have to fight to maintain my
balance.

To reach the American Hut only takes an hour, the
shortest of all our treks. We are now based at a height
of about 4,500 metres (15,000 feet), so there is only
another 600 metres (2,000 ft) to climb. We set out the
tents for the final time, and camp well within the sight
of the Ice Wall of Mt Kenya. I can gaze up at the Ice
Diamond and the Ice Couloir. The aptly named Gate of
Mists is set between them, all very formidable looking
indeed. I can see the several routes that we can attempt
the next morning; none of them look easy, and we will
need to ice-axe our way up them. One of the team has
left us, to take a trek to the Mombasa coast, and the rest
of us are to split into two parties; five will walk and trek
around the perimeter of Mt Kenya, while the remaining
four, the three most experienced climbers and myself,
will set off this afternoon to try and reach the summit.
The plan is to leave our tents at the American Hut and
then bivi on the mountain that night to enable us to
make for the summit very early the following morning.
This is as far as the porters will go; it will be now up to
the four of us to carry whatever food and equipment we

will need, and to decide the best route and how we are to attempt the climb.

Near the American Hut is a group, almost a semi-circle, of stones, with a long narrow stone in front. It makes me think that perhaps once it was set up to create an ancient sundial. The stones are a fitting tribute to those who, over the centuries, have passed this way before and who have stood, as we now stand, at the foot of an exceptional mountain that itself is timeless, more or less unaffected by the strife and tribulation that we humans experience. Simple words from a Zen master to his student reveal the essence of this place: 'Where are you going?' 'I go where it is changeless.' 'How can you go where it is changeless?' 'My going creates no change.' As if to emphasise our lack of importance to the scene the hyrax constantly appear to mock and observe us, then, as mysteriously, disappear, only to re-appear suddenly, poised on another rocky section. There are numerous small birds that gradually become emboldened, hopping around the tents and even between us, trying to pick up particles of food. We know we are waiting for the moment to arrive. It will be soon.

At 4.00 pm we decide that the four of us should now set off. Edwin has been concerned about me throughout, and has always tried to lessen the strains on my knee by carrying as much of my equipment as possible and trying to guide me through the coarser terrain on to easier paths. He volunteers to carry my backpack to the bivi site. The way is steep and harsh, and we climb very slowly. It is an extremely painful process, particularly for me, and the pressure on my knee is severe. We climb between decaying trees and over heavily-packed mosses, following paths that are constantly wet and slippery. We have to clamber over sharp-edged rocks that have fallen from the peaks, and often they move under our feet – very unnerving for me, and I have to steady myself to prevent myself from falling. After several hours we reach the final bivi area, set perfectly within an enclosed rock gully, just below the Ice Diamond route. Edwin places my pack on the rocks and returns to our tents far below. Long afterwards I can still remember the concern deep in his eyes.

In fact there is a small tin sleeping hut built into the rocks but we all prefer to bivi outside on this final night. We choose our positions, and lay out our bivi bags and sleeping bags. I am conscious of those who have been here before us. The rocks and the ice seem full of sparkling lights. I am extremely cold, even though I have put on all the extra clothes I have with me, but I am even more worried about the worsening condition of my knee and how it will react to the intense pressures it will have to endure on the final ice climbs. We boil soup and tea, and eat bars of chocolate, mentally trying to ready ourselves for the coming day. The silence is overpowering and soon cuts through and ceases our nervous chatter. It seems most appropriate that this area is known as the Black Hole Bivi.

Next morning, after only a few hours rest but little sleep, I get up at approximately 3.30 am. In the half-light there are many dancing shadows and movements. It is like being in some other existence, passing through one world into another. I can feel the ghosts of the mountains and the ghosts of past climbers, and I can't tell whether they are warning me away or encouraging me on. We decide to leave behind our bivi bags, sleeping bags and walking boots, as they won't be needed again until our return. I lace up my climbing boots, strap on the head torch, and load up my backpack with all the water I have, my spare clothes and most of my food. The air is thin and fiercely crisp, yet I enjoy the taste of it for it is full of life and energy. I determine to do my best. The four of us wish each other good luck and godspeed, and I guess that each of us says a silent prayer.

The way is littered with stones and boulders, which

I can't help stumbling over. They are twisted into different shapes and sizes, trying, it seems, to block our way. Both my legs feel so heavy, weighted down and cumbersome. All the time my right knee is subjected to tremendous strains as I gingerly try to manoeuvre my legs up and over the rocks. After a short but very arduous climb we reach the area of the Ice Window and the Ice Couloir.

I rope myself to John Barry, and Jim McWilliams ropes himself to Dave Halton. We continue the climb in our two teams. We stop for a few moments, and I put on my helmet, fix the boot crampons and grip my two small ice axes. We have to continue using the head torches as it is still dark. The way ahead at first looks absolutely sheer, but I then see that there are a few places to hold on to if you lean right into the mountain. Barry and I are the leading climbers, with Halton and McWilliams shortly behind us. I am trying to use the crampon spikes to dig into the ice and grip more firmly. Barry had hoped there would be some softer and crisper ice on the couloir into which we could step more easily, particularly using our crampons, but there is only black ice as hard as the rock itself. It continues to frustrate my efforts with my crampon spikes. It becomes more difficult to put any pressure on my right knee, and I struggle unsuccessfully to maintain a reasonable momentum. I have to stop more and more often because of the pain, and am obviously in great trouble.

Barry decides to climb on alone to test out the conditions, and asks me to wait behind with the others. When he is some 15 metres (50 ft) above us he belays a rope down and calls out to me to attach it to my belt so that he can help me to climb up the sheer ice wall. The other two climbers stop and wait to watch my progress. Barry first climbs across the ice rim, edging his way to its left, and there hammers in an iron piton to provide support for the rope and my weight. He shouts for me to follow the route he has taken, to climb slowly up the first section and then to edge across to join him. I cannot see a clear and easy way to go, but, after some hesitation, start off as he suggests. I know that one must be willing to drown, and I also know that fear is the first and foremost hindrance to going deeper when committing oneself to anything. I must climb and go higher, much higher. There is no other way. I breath in strongly and start up the wall.

I have managed some 5 metres when my knee starts to fail. It gives way so that I cannot kick my right foot into the ice any longer. It seems to have lost all strength, and refuses to obey my insistent demands on it. I cannot hold on, and start falling. The rope whips across the ice, slowing my fall and just holds me to the mountain. As it is fixed across to the left of the ice rim I cannot help but fall in that direction. I start sliding across the ice wall, gaining momentum at an alarming rate. I try to halt the slide and stop myself and stab into the ice with the small hand axes, but without any success. My whole body is banging against the black ice all the time, my chest and arms thumping into it, but I hardly feel the pain, suffering more from the total fear of being absolutely out of control. I can see the rocks on the left side of the mountain looming closer and closer as I move relentlessly towards them, gathering speed. I realise I will crash into them at any moment and re-double my efforts to halt my progress. The other two climbers below me and to the right of me can only watch in horror, knowing they can do nothing to help. The battle is my own. I struggle to grip myself into the ice and slow my speed, and somehow I succeed. I stop less than a metre short of the rocks, and just avoid crashing into them.

The rope is at full stretch and I am hanging on it, leaning into the mountain, trying to recover from my ordeal and balance myself on my left crampon. My right elbow is totally bruised and the condition of my right knee is indescribable; it feels totally without support, one long deep hurting. I hang and rest there for some very weary moments before trying to pull myself together, gain some strength and decide what to do next. There is no way the two climbers on my right can climb across the hardened ice of the mountain wall to reach me. Barry is positioned way up above me, helping to support the rope, and it would be an almost impossible, let alone unfair, task to expect him to climb down and help me. There is a *koan* that seems to sum it all up: 'No matter what you say or do, life may end to-night.' There is really no choice. I mouth to myself the Zen shout 'Katsu'. This cannot be translated; it has no literal meaning, being a sound of mental commitment and continuance.

I have to climb again. I inch myself up slowly, using my arms, the ice axes and the crampons to dig in as best I can. It is completely exhausting and I have to stop every few feet. There is no other way and I continue my slow and painful ascent as best I can, resting every few minutes. It seems to take for ever. Perhaps only 30 minutes pass, but they feel like the longest minutes I have ever known. I can sense the deep anxiety of the others as they watch my ultra-slow, cautious, deliberate actions. The ice axes sometimes lock themselves into the ice and are extremely difficult to dislodge, but eventually I am able to reach Barry, waiting anxiously and impatiently for me at a rock overhang. Utterly exhausted, I lodge myself into the rocks and we wait there for McWilliams and Halton to make their own laborious way up to join us. We are now 5,000 metres (16,500 ft). After some deliberations Barry decides that the black ice makes it impossible for us to continue to the summit, just a tantalising 150 metres (500 ft) above us. He feels we are likely to end up with a major accident. As a team we agree to descend.

The easiest way down, and certainly the fastest, although just as painful for me, is to abseil. Halton leads and I follow, then McWilliams and finally Barry. The abseils down the mountain are made in 30- to 45-metre (100- to 150-ft) sections. I have the one experience of mountain abseiling, on my ascent of Mont Blanc, but I follow the instructions closely and manage to work my way down, section by section. Each time I plant my feet apart, letting out the lead rope through the figure-of-eight metal loop and edge downwards. In fact I realise that this way is actually much easier on my legs and knees than it would have been climbing down. However there are some nerve-wracking moments, particularly when the four of us have to perch together on a tiny ice-ledge, all of us standing upright and holding to the ice and rocks for support before the next abseil stage can be organised. However, the four of us are able to take each other's weight; I realise that on my own or with just one other climber it would be very dangerous indeed.

Finally we reach an ice levée. Now I can step more easily either sideways or downwards, though still wearing my ice crampons. The best way with crampons is to step forward directly down the mountain, but I have no confidence in my knee, which continually feels as if it might give way again. Fear is the greatest obstacle, the remedy always being perseverance. Eventually we reach the bottom, remove our crampons and start to make our way back to the bivi camp. I then step on to a loose rock, my knee gives way completely and I scream out. It is several moments before the pain subsides and I can continue.

At the bivi camp we prepare some very welcome hot food and drinks. Halton and McWilliams decide to bivi there one more night and to make a final attempt on the summit the next morning. Barry and I continue our way down to the American Hut, although I am soon a long way behind him. It is a painful and laborious descent. I have to search each time for a secure rock on which to plant my feet, in order not to put too much strain on my knee. It feels completely swollen, and the throbbing and pain is a constant reminder of what I have put it through. Edwin has been keeping watch for us at the lower camp. When he sees us descending he comes up to meet us, and helps me to carry down my pack. I climb inside my tent and am soon asleep from sheer utter exhaustion, even though it is only 2.00 pm. After a while the other climbers return from their trek around the mountain, and I wake up to tell them of the saga and how near we got to the top. Barry shares with me my keen disappointment and suggests the two of us attempt Point Lenana, the third highest peak of Mt Kenya, the next morning. I don't think I can or should try anything further. He asks me to sleep on it and decide the next morning, but I don't expect I will change my mind. I feel even more disappointed with my disappointment than with our not reaching the summit together. I feel I have become one-track minded, and that is not the way. I have understood 'the one in the many' but not 'the many in the one.' I recall a *koan* to balance myself: 'All humans are subject to the natural course of life (the snow covers a thousand hills).'

13

The Third Summit

During the night I sleep fitfully, restless and uneasy. When I do manage to sleep I dream vividly, strange ferocious adventures mostly involving Shakespeare, Oscar Wilde and Queen Victoria, nothing about mountains. At around 4.00 am I am suddenly wide awake, and from then on I cannot get back to sleep again. Eventually I decide to get up at 6.00 am. John Barry is also awake, and pops his head out of his tent to ask me again do I want to try and climb another mountain summit, to Point Lenana? My legs and head say definitely no, but surprisingly my heart (or perhaps it's my *shin* speaking) agrees and I quickly finish dressing, pack my water and camera and prepare myself. Edwin arrives just before 7.00 am and is willing to lead us. He's a real champion, and I am indebted to him. The three of us start out on the trek and climb. What have I agreed to do! Will my legs stand up to it? I will shortly find out.

The initial stage is a very long slow struggle, clambering over all kinds of vegetation and rocks, until we reach the main climbing sections. There we head for the first ridge, just to the right of the Kenyan peaks. It is populated with various trees and bushes and short stumpy palms, many with broken and dying roots.

In progressing towards Point Lenana it is necessary

to scramble up the very large scree slope to the left of Shipton's Peak, where the path starts zigzagging upwards. The path eventually reaches the crest of a small ridge, where the huge expanse of the Louis Glacier can be clearly and dramatically seen. Beyond the glacier is the imposing South-East face of the Nelion peak, looking absolutely spectacular in the early morning light. The gradient eases slightly as the path trails left (north-east) across a small rocky plateau.

After our climb of that first ridge we then have to descend sharply to another valley floor in order to reach the next ridge. This is composed mostly of small rocks, gravel and loose scree. These surfaces are very jarring on my knees, but I find I can continue. It is a very long haul up that slope, but eventually I make it. Then we come to a snow and ice section that we will have to traverse. Fortunately this is not the black ice of yesterday; it is crunchier, and I can push my boots into it more easily. We complete the ice traverse and reach the Austrian Hut. From there the summit of Point Lenana is clearly visible to the right of the Louis Glacier, the path taking us straight towards it. I keep to the rocks where possible, trying to avoid the loose slippery scree that causes me pain. Where it can be found I trudge across the patches of snow and ice.

We have now climbed about halfway to Point Lenana. I keep my pace steady, and manage to achieve a constant rhythm. This walking meditation is called *kinhin*. It is preferable – necessary really – to cup one's hands, holding them over one's *hara*, to 'try to keep the feet warm and the head cool'.

A number of early climbers are already making their way down, and we exchange greetings. After some further steady progress, during which I surprise myself with my ability to keep going, the end of the climb is in sight. I scramble over, and sometimes between, the noble rocks. To reach the summit itself, at the very end of the ascent, it is necessary to scale a rock wall about chest high. With one knee unable to take my weight or any real strain, I reach upwards with my arms, grasp some protruding stones and pull myself over the top. There are just a few more yards to scramble across, and I have reached the summit of Point Lenana. A few simple posts mark the peak. There is also a separate and poignant dedication to a British schoolmaster who died on the mountain; it seems he loved Mt Kenya so much that a special plaque in his memory was financed and fixed to a rock by one of the Rotary Clubs.

The views here are truly magnificent. We can see many of the different routes up Mt Kenya, as well as the glorious valleys and terrains stretching far into the distance on all sides. There are the Austrian and Top Huts and the head of the Teleki Valley. Across the Louis and Gregory Glaciers are Point Thomson and the two main summits of Nelion and Batian, although both are partially obscured by rock faces. Further to the right (north-west) Mackinder's Valley can be seen, while turning again to the right (north-east) the Gorges Valley, Hall Tarns and the precipice of The Temple, are clearly visible. I am told that on very clear mornings one can see the peaks of Kilimanjaro and Mawenzi, way above the clouds, over 350 km (200 miles) to the south.

I am thrilled to have managed this third summit, and am grateful to Barry for suggesting it and persuading me to attempt it. As he says, two out of three summits isn't too bad, particularly as we were only some 150 metres from the summit of the second one. I learn that Lenana is named after one of the great Masai warriors, and feel a little bit like one myself. Perhaps one shout is permissible. The sound reverberates and is full of sweetness. We can only live life for each moment. Perhaps we are too concerned with the past. It has gone forever, while the future is still only a hope and a prayer. I think a prayer of thanks is justified, and imagine that everyone who makes it to this point feels the same.

After a short rest it is time to go down. I lower myself gingerly off the rock wall and start my descent. It took us just over two hours from the American Hut to reach the summit, which I'm told is quite a fast time, certainly for someone whose legs were in my condition. I guess it is because I am not suffering any altitude problems and can therefore keep up a regular pace without having to stop at all. Going down, however, I have to maintain that same pace, again concentrating on each of my steps and trying to make certain that I do not wrench my knee. This requires dedicated concentration, and is very sapping. I feel myself weakening rapidly. The scree feels unstable underfoot, and I have to move very cautiously, trying to plant each foot securely.

I finally make it across the scree slopes and enter a small dense forest of giant groundsels. The giant groundsel forests are a rarity on Mt Kenya; usually the groundsel only grows singly, and far apart. Stems of these weird-looking plants grow so close together that sometimes, as I pass amongst them, they hide the sight of the sky and the mountain from me. Some trees, many more than 5 metres high, have grown so closely together that they have died, but remain there standing, rotting, propped up, one leaning against another.

Beyond the groundsels I come across swampy marsh-land, camouflaged by a bright green moss. The moss itself is dotted with buttercups, as well as a very interesting plant whose leaves form a scalloped cup, actually sunk into the moss itself, at the bottom of which is a yellow flower. I later discover this is known as *Arctotis rueppelil*. Throughout the climb and the trek, particularly on the lower slopes, I often come across the gorgeous helichrysum, its wonderful name being derived from the Greek *helios*, meaning sun, and *chrysos*, meaning gold.

At the American Hut everyone is waiting for us and we all celebrate our triumphs by trying to finish off as much of the food as we can, knowing that we won't need it again. I am so weary, but at the same time feel very content that I managed this third and last summit. We wait anxiously for the return of Halton and McWilliams and their news. Unfortunately after some hours they return with horrifying stories of being assailed by numerous rock falls brought on by shifting snows. As the day had progressed the hot sun had taken command and loosened the higher ice section, and the way had become impassable. They had some lucky escapes as they quickly abseiled back down. There is little else to do for the rest of the day except rest, read and write in our diaries. We all need to try to recoup, to gather our strengths. After a final meal and clearing up the camp site it is time to go to bed. I sleep far better this night, knowing that my mountains are over and that it has been a successful expedition for all the team members. Each in his or her way has accomplished enough to have made it worthwhile.

The next day I am up very early and load up my backpack. I want to be the first to set off and commence the trek down. I descend, as always, with Edwin. We pass Mackinder's and the other huts and head down through the marshes. It is a long slow process but I don't mind, now the pressure is off. From Teleki Lodge, Shipton's Peak with its pointed summit and steep west face is clearly visible at the head of the valley. To the right of the peak is a large quarry carved into a bowl-shaped depression. Teleki Tarn is at the base of this quarry. We follow the path from Teleki Lodge down to the valley floor, passing below and to the right of the Mountain Club of Kenya Hut. We cross a few small streams and another boggy section before aiming for the lowest point in the U-shaped lip at the open side of the quarry. A waterfall flows over the left side of the lip and the path goes up a small scree slope to the right of the waterfall, to the edge of the lip, then drops to reach the tarn. It is clear how far we have climbed in order to make our ascents.

As we continue downwards I meet a number of climbers climbing up. They are making really slow progress and straining with the effort necessary to continue even on the lower ridges. But for us there are beautiful landscapes to savour, and the air is fresh and exhilarating. There are also plenty of rock hyrax to be seen, on the tops of boulders, on rocks and other high vantage points, silently staring at us. Magnificent huge trees are bent over with the weight of sweeping trailing vines and thick foliage. My legs, although so tired, seem to know the way to go, and after many hours walking Edwin and I reach the meteorological station. There there are several groups of tame monkeys, almost approachable, frolicking around the grass areas. I would like to linger, but the jeeps are waiting. I am the last to arrive, and we load up and head quickly back to the Naro Moro Lodge. There we pick up the items and clothes we left behind, and enjoy a final celebratory meal.

We have to decide where to stay the next night, so I make contact with an old friend, Charles Szlapak, who owns the Fairview Hotel in Nairobi. The hotel has bedrooms, as is normal for a hotel, but for each of us this is a tremendous luxury. However the greatest pleasure we derive is in taking a long hot bath. I submerge myself so just my eyes and mouth are above the water line, and feel the layers of dirt and grime slowly wash off and float away. I empty the bath twice and refill it until finally I accept that I am thoroughly clean. It is 31 December, the last day of the year, and the manager of the hotel makes certain that we have a wonderful meal and an interesting evening. We stay up late to toast in the first day of a brand new year. It is particularly special to all of us.

Despite only a few hours sleep we are up early, missing out on breakfast, ready to load our baggage and equipment into the coach. It takes us directly to Nairobi airport, where we have to fly to Dar-es-Salaam before making our connection back to London.

I am at peace. Everything has its place in life; we are all part of the whole. I was on a mountain, on two mountains, on many mountains. Those that haven't climbed can still belong to the mountain, just as the mountain belongs to them: 'An ant can still look at a mountain.' I remember another *koan* that simply states a great truth: 'On Mt Hakone there is the man riding in the sedan chair. There is the one who pulls the sedan chair. And there is the one who makes the straw sandals of the one pulling the sedan chair.'

Once again I have learned the necessity of climbing with the mind as well as with the body. The great religions teach us that there are three sacred elements of experience – time, place, and the soul – and I have found all three. By making him aware of silence, a Zen master initially prepares and opens his student to the experience of being. These two great African mountains have reinforced the essential role that such silence should have within our lives. Additionally, the four supreme emotions – loving kindness, compassion, joy, tranquillity – are to be found on the mountains in abundance. I was fortunate to have my share of these, due in no small part to the comradeship and inspiration of my fellow climbers and our heroic African guides. I will always carry with me the memories of Mt Kilimanjaro and Mt Kenya, the highest and most magnificent in all Africa. They are there, I was there and I am still there.

Glossary

bivouac (bivi) To sleep outside. A bivi bag is used to cover the sleeping bag.

ch'an The Chinese word derived from the Sanskrit word *dhyana*, translating in Japanese to Zen.

dharma (dhamma) A Sanskrit word to express the laws of liberation and of nature.

do The Way.

dohyo The place (ring) particularly used for contests in Sumo.

dojo Any place where meditation is practised.

dukkha The integral pain that each human being carries in one form or another; also that part of each person which remains unsatisfied.

hara The source of energy located in the lower abdomen, used as a focus in Zen meditation.

hishiryo The consciousness occurring beyond thought, without the effort of thinking.

ji The skill and technical aspects of a Zen art, also meaning a fact or an object.

jiki jitsu Supervising teacher in charge of meditation.

joriki The power of concentrating the mind, relying on one's own efforts.

judo Originally known as *ju-jutsu*. This is a form of wrestling applying the principles of Taoism and Zen. It uses the opponent's strength against himself.

karma This is a Sanskrit word, its root derived from the word for action, and has come to mean action and the results of such action. Every living thing results from the karmic effect of the positive or negative actions of the previous moment and is the cause of the following moment. Constant rebirth occurs, therefore creating new chances.

karuna One of the four supreme emotions, expressing compassion. (Can also be a process that develops slowly.)

katsu No literal meaning, but used as a shout to summon up one's strengths and commitment, or even to frighten and deter an opponent.

keisaku (*kyosaku*) A light flat stick used to strike students who are losing concentration or who need stimulating.

kendo The way of the sword.

kensho A way of seeing deep into one's own nature. It creates the opportunity to experience *satori*, and is sometimes considered its equivalent.

ki The innate force that flows within each person, as well as in the cosmos.

kinhin A way of meditating whilst walking.

koan A word, riddle or statement, sometimes paradoxical, which cannot be easily understood or resolved with the intellect but needs intuitive thought and comprehension. It is used as an exercise to stimulate the mind and to break the limitations of ordinary thought.

kontin A state within *zazen* when the practitioner is experiencing drowsiness.

kyudo The way of the bow.

mantra A repetitive word or statement used to concentrate the mind and a person's energies.

metta One of the four supreme emotions, expressing loving-kindness.

mondo The short dialogues entered into by Zen master and student to arouse thought and intuition.

mu Japanese word meaning not, or nothing, or expressing the negative. An answer to silence a question.

mudita One of the four supreme emotions, expressing joy. Coupled with a feeling of sympathy, altruistic joy.

mushin Emptying the mind; the state of nothingness aspired to in *zazen*.

nirvana (*nibbana*) The absolute state, whereby all desire is removed.

niwazume The period of waiting and endurance undertaken by Zen novices before being allowed to receive Zen instruction. It can be a few years or stretch to several years and is a real test of willingness and commitment.

nyaga (*ngai*) Masai word for God.

prajna Wisdom transcending knowledge itself, thereby achieving divine intuition.

ri The underlying principles of the universe; inspiration; universal truths. Peak (Tibetan).

Rinzai Zen One of the two main schools of Zen practice, founded by Master Rinzai. It is a very vigorous form, relying considerably on *koan* and *mondo*, following directly from the teachings of Hui-Neng.

ryu The traditions of the *Samurai*.

sando The way of the mountain.

sankhara Our mental or karmic formations.

Samurai The Japanese warrior trained to the highest degree to follow the principles of honour and bravery. Meaning 'those who serve'.

satori The enlightenment sought after by all those undergoing intense meditation. It is the awakening to the ultimate truth.

sesshin A period of time during which *zazen* is intensively carried out. Also a meditation retreat.

shin The mental spirit, the mind; the inner power summoned in combat and to contest any great mental or physical obstacles encountered.

skandas (*khandas*) The five parts comprising the whole: body, feeling, perception, conception (also known as mental formations), consciousness.

Soto Zen One of the two main schools of Zen practice founded by Master Dogen. It is more reflective than Rinzai Zen, quieter, and rarely uses *koans* as part of its teachings.

t'ai chi A method of slow movements to concentrate energies and inner forces. It can be a form of combat without using weapons.

tanden The centre of the *hara*; also the centre of a person, either physically or psychologically.

thriki Relying on the efforts of others.

thumo reskiang The mental process of raising the body's temperature.

upekkha One of the four supreme emotions, expressing the tranquillity of spirit, equanimity.

wasa Technique, skill.

zanshin Carrying the *shin*, the inner strengths and forces, from one action through to the next and thereafter.

zazen Literally meaning Zen-sitting; practising Zen in its concentrated form.

Zen Translated from *ch'an* which in turn is translated from *dhyana*, meaning, in its basic form, meditation. It is a way, some would say the Way, of liberating the mind and allowing it to achieve its fullest potential.

zendo The hall or building used for the practice of Zen.

Appendix 1

Letter from the Physiotherapist of
The Remedial Dance Clinic

The Remedial Dance Clinic
78 Harley Street London W1N 1AE Telephone: 071-580 1650
DANCE AND SPORTS INJURIES CLINIC

KDC/SG

30 January 1992

Mr N Shulman
National Children's Home
4 St George's House
15 Hanover Square
London
W1R 9AJ

Dear Mr Shulman

We refer to our treatments of your ruptured right knee ligament over
recent weeks after the damage caused in the accident on December 5 1991.

At that time when we learned of your undertaking to climb the
highest mountains in Africa in mid December for Charity, we had no
choice but to advise you to cancel the expedition, as there seemed
no way your knee could stand up to the rigours of mountain climbing.

After your decision to proceed wearing a knee brace to provide some
support, we still thought it unwise for you to go ahead and very
unlikely you would be able to climb.

On your return we were surprised but delighted to learn you had
not only successfully climbed to the Summit of Kilimanjaro,
over 19,000 feet, but additionally Mount Kenya and Point Lenana,
over 16,000 feet each. With a wasted knee muscle the only way you
could achieve such strenuous activities was your absolute personal
determination, really a clear question of mind over matter.

It is now very important that you now allow your knee to recover
fully before undertaking anything further.

Best wishes

Yours sincerely

Sally Geater RGRT MCSP SRP
Physiotherapist

Justin Howse F.R.C.S. Shirley Hancock M.C.S.P., S.R.P.

The Remedial Dance Clinic Ltd. Reg. in England No. 1691567 Gresham House, 53 Clarendon Road, Watford, Herts. WD1 1LR

Appendix 2

Letter from the Expedition Leader, John Barry

Neville Shulman

16 January 1992

Dear Neville,

I write to congratulate you:
two – and very nearly three – of Africa's highest mountains on one-and-a-half legs! I've soldiered through thick and thin and have climbed on thin and thick these last twenty years, but never have I witnessed a more inspiring display of dogged determination – of sheer guts.

How you hauled yourself up on that last day – the last of five such days – on the Machame Route on Kilimanjaro (19,340 feet), that endless last 4,000 feet, on one good leg, is still a source of wonder to me. It hurt just to watch and to listen. I was tired on two legs. No wonder your doctors find it hard to credit: no wonder they cried impossible before and cried again, impossible, after. On the soberest reflection it is hard to believe – and I was there! It was a great moment standing there with you on the top of all Africa.

My plan for Mt. Kenya didn't quite work – but only by a few hundred feet. If you'll (painfully) recall, Mt. Kenya (17,038 feet), is a technically difficult mountain with no easy way, up or down. I gambled that the Ice Window route, though a steep and serious ice climb of fifteen hundred feet, would put less strain and cause less pain to your leg than the steep scramble on Kilimanjaro or than any of the alternative – and still hard – rock routes on Mt. Kenya. And I still hold that the plan would have worked had the short rains deposited their customary snow cover. As it turned out, there had been no short rains that year, so that we were confronted by a thin and dangerous seam of black ice rather than by the friendly blanket of white snow-ice it was reasonable to expect. Even so, we were but 500 feet from the Gate of the Mists when I sounded the retreat. You wouldn't quit, but I simply couldn't bear to be party to your suffering any longer. If sponsorship was awarded in direct proportion to effort, then the National Children's Home would now be the best funded charity on this earth. I know that you were loath to beat a retreat, but Grade 4 ice-climbing with a knee full of wrecked ligaments and contained in a brace didn't seem an equal struggle even for charity. I was mindful too of the long term damage I might have been encouraging. Later, abseiling down that black ice through fusillades of stonefall and sensing your disappointment, I conceived a plan B: that if on the morrow your leg still worked at all – which didn't look likely – then we could climb to Point Lenana (16,355 feet), Africa's third summit and often claimed by those who have climbed it as an ascent of Mt. Kenya – which, to purists like ourselves, it isn't quite. And so the next day, with rather less than three-and-a-half legs between us, we took it by storm. The view of Kilimanjaro far off to the South, and of Mt. Kenya just next door to the North (and only the littlest bit nearer the sky), seemed just reward: it was a good place to be.

And now so sure am I that given *either* two good legs, *or* decent snow conditions, we would have triumphed. I am suggesting that we return, after the long rains and finish what we came so close to achieving: knock off Point Batian, Kenya's highest summit.

Truly you were brilliant

Yours aye,

JOHN BARRY
DIRECTOR, SURVIVAL CLUB

Appendix 3

No Surrender by David Halton

Tanzania

From the moment JB asked me to help him organise a trip to get Neville Shulman to the summits of Mount Kilimanjaro and Mt Kenya, in order to raise money for the National Childrens Homes – George Thomas Society – I had no doubt that John would succeed in getting the job entrusted to him done. Two years ago he said he would carry Neville to the top of Mont Blanc to raise fifty thousand pounds but he didn't. Neville stormed it.

The prospects of John having to carry physically Neville seemed to loom close to reality when only two weeks before the trip, Neville rang to say that he was considering cancelling the effort. He explained that he had been running and tripped tearing several ligaments in his knee and quite rightly thought the injury would make the challenge impossible. John would hear nothing of this and was sure that we could still succeed, although it may take a little longer.

Our climb was to take us through rain forests, alpine meadows, lost valleys and across snow fields, up slimy, boot gobbling, root infested mud paths and over colcanic moranes, leading eventually around a wind swept frozen crater rim to the roof of Africa. Would Neville's knee take the abuse it would inevitably receive? As we set off up through the jungle he was in fine form and when we arrived at our first camp some six hours later he seemed very confident. During that five hours it rained so hard it made your head hurt.

After four days we were at the Barafu hut, which consisted of two small boxes perched on a ridge. We had endured some long days; one had been a scenic diversion by our guide, who failed to realise that our vision was somewhat restricted by the mists, and that standing in a fogged our 'lost valley' was not quite what we had in mind, especially when the detour had taken us some four hours longer than the standard route, and had greatly added to the fatigue of Neville's knee. Admittedly the valley from what we saw was beautifully prehistoric and would have been a photographers dream if we had been able to see it all. So we could not really be angry with him, as he had only tried to show us his discovery. To reach the Barafu hut we had also encountered some fine scrambling and some hard slogs but we were now only day's climb from the summit and Neville was going well. His knee was holding out, even though he had twisted it badly a couple of times, which I am sure the whole of Africa must have known about it, as on these occurrences he cried out with pain. He and couple of others were also feeling the altitude and felt a bit sickly as they bedded down in the drafty box.

It was to be a short night as we were to rise at midnight to start the haul up to the summit. We shook ourselves from our sleeping bags when the new day started and stumbled around in the dark, with the anticipation growing. Would Neville make it? We all wished each other luck and made off into the moonlit night on what was to be a twenty-hour day.

I led my group ahead of John's which included Neville. Neville was much slower than us and we soon left them behind as we snailed our way up the scree and snow slopes. It was cold, very cold and the pace was not really fast enough to keep us all warm. The altitude started to get the better of the heaving lungs and pounding heads.

We all rested and looked down the couloir. There was no sign of John and Neville. Then, very faintly, we could hear the ringing of an ice axe drifting up out of the gloom and knew Neville was still plugging away. We started chanting louder and louder 'Come on Neville, come on Neville'. In the early morning light and the still, early gloom, the ghostly echos rang out their encouragement all around us. Slowly but surely the ringing of his axe got closer, we resumed our vocal encouragement and sure enough Neville's deliberate and methodical steps brought him into view for a moment. Then the mists engulfed him again. Cold and tired my group decided to head off down the ridge on the long walk to the Horombo hut, but I could not leave. I was rooted to the spot, I had to know if Neville had made it all the way. I crouched, sat on my haunches and waited. The sight I eventually saw was one of the most humbling I had ever seen. I could see the pain in every determined step Neville took etched deep on his grimaced face. It was agonizing for me to watch. His deliberate and precise gait brought him nearer – his determination was awesome.

He arrived at the col exhausted and cold. 'Not much further' I told him. He looked up at me in disbelief, then managed to turn the corners of his mouth up in a vain attempt to smile. He struggled to his feet and gingerly took another step toward the summit. JB and the rest of his team – Jim the American, and the youngest member Stephen Furnell followed me, as I retraced my footsteps back to the summit for the second time – I had to see Neville at the top.

One hours trudge later and I pushed Neville to the front, and he led the last few metres to the summit. I was totally consumed by the extraordinary human effort that Neville had shown in getting there and am very proud to have witnessed his truly superhuman effort in reaching the first half of his goal.

Kenya

We had kept to the tight schedule so far, but I had serious doubts about being able to do the route and make it back to the hotel in the three days we had left. We all slept like logs that night, catching up on the previous days lack of it. The final push up through the glacial debris to the black hole bivouac the next day, saw us positions for an Alpine start on the route the next morning. There were only four of us now.

The rest had gone off to walk the summit circuit and climb to point Lenana. John would lead Neville up the route and I would lead Jim, the American club member of the team. By four o'clock the next morning we where at the foot of the climb. John led off up the steep couloir. As it got steeper and we got higher, the ice got harder. Neville was plugging away with his slow methodical rhythm upward when a misplaced crampon caused him to stumble and fall on the rope. John held his slip, and I helped him back to his feet. The ice was 45 degrees and we were still moving together, rather than pitching it, so after Neville had regained his feet John dropped his coils of rope and headed off up to the headwall to arrange a belay.

The sun was starting to creep over the horizon as we all stood under the head wall. We had climbed a thousand feet of ice, but this was where the real climbing would start. John again led the route up a pitch across the couloir and up to the next stance. Neville moved off, his progress was slow. We were quite concerned about the rock fall and encouraged Neville to try and get across the stone fall line as quickly as he could. I was concentrating on getting my rope sorted out ready to lead off when I heard the clatter of plastic boots – if you have ever been unfortunate enough to hear anyone falling with plastic boots on, then it is a sound that you never wish to hear again, but it is a sound that once heard is never forgotten – Neville was falling. He pendulumed across the couloir some hundred feet, John holding him on the rope. He eventually came to a rest none the worse for wear, but understandably a little shaken. But once again Neville's determination lifted him to his crampon points and once again he began to wield his axes. The movement of his injured leg was virtually nil and he resembled a small child on his very first venture up a flight of stairs – one step at a time – he clung on to his axes as if they were a banister. It was painful to watch him, but slowly he hauled himself up to John's stance.

By the time Jim and I had climbed the pitch John had made the decision to go back down. He could no longer watch Neville go through any more pain, knowing full well that the harder part of the route was to come. We took the odd photo at our high point and then retreated back down to the bivi site. Jim and I made the decision to have another crack at the route the following day.

By 6AM the following morning we had reached our previous day's high point and were going well. The following move from the ledge was a very exposed traverse on rotten ice around a rock bulge into the couloir. The final straw came when we were one pitch short of the ice window itself, I placed an ice screw only to find the ice hollow. As I withdrew my hand from the screw a plug of ice blew out of the end and a gush of water started to pour out – it was just as if I had drilled a lead pipe. That was the turning point, with Jim slowing down and the rock falls increasing I made the decision to retreat.

We eventually made it down, and walked into camp a little disillusioned at failing the route, as we did not have time for a third attempt. What did cheer us up no end was to see Neville's face beaming, he and John had made Point Lenana at sun rise that morning, thus fulfilling his goal of getting to the top of Africa's two highest peaks.

Appendix 4
Copy of the Kilimanjaro National Park Certificate Confirming the Climb to Uhuru Peak, the Summit of Kilimanjaro

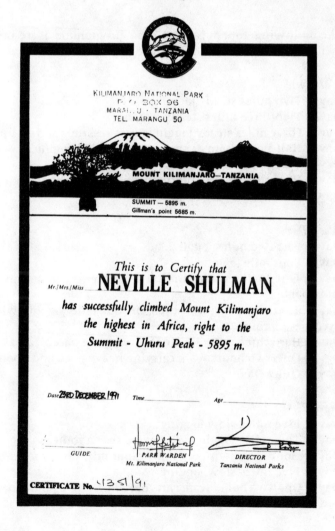

KILIMANJARO NATIONAL PARK
P. O. BOX 96
MARANGU · TANZANIA
TEL. MARANGU 50

MOUNT KILIMANJARO—TANZANIA

SUMMIT — 5895 m.
Gillman's point 5685 m.

This is to Certify that

Mr./Mrs./Miss **NEVILLE SHULMAN**

has successfully climbed Mount Kilimanjaro the highest in Africa, right to the Summit - Uhuru Peak - 5895 m.

Date 23RD DECEMBER 1991   Time   Age

....   GUIDE

PARK WARDEN
Mt. Kilimanjaro National Park

DIRECTOR
Tanzania National Parks

CERTIFICATE No. 1351/91

Appendix 5

Fitness Training Programme

The following four-week training programme is recommended and certainly will produce substantial benefits.

Week One
Day 1: Two miles steady jogging.
Day 2: Two/three miles steady jogging.
Day 3: Three miles steady jogging plus press-ups and sit-ups.
Day 4: Half-hour swim or cycle or three mile jogging.
Day 5: Three-mile run with exercises en route.
Day 6: Hard three miles, alternatively sprinting and jogging.
Day 7: Quiet Day.

Week Two
Day 1: Fast two miles jogging.
Day 2: Four mile jogging.
Day 3: One hour's walk carrying a twenty-five pound pack and boots.
Day 4: Hour-long swim or cycle or four-mile jogging with exercises en route.
Day 5: Hard three miles jogging, varying the pace.
Day 6: One/two hours walk carrying heavy pack and boots.
Day 7: Quiet Day.

Week Three
Day 1: Five miles slow jogging.
Day 2: Two miles jogging with exercises en route.
Day 3: Hour-long swim or cycle or four mile fast run.
Day 4: Five miles slow jogging.
Day 5: One/two hours walk carrying a thirty-five pound pack and boots.

Day 6: Four miles hard running.
Day 7: Quiet Day.

Week Four
Day 1: One/two hours walk carrying a forty-pound pack and boots.
Day 2: Five miles running, varying the pace and exercises en route.
Day 3: One hour swim or cycle or four miles jogging.
Day 4: Five miles slow jogging.
Day 5: Six to eight miles jogging.
Day 6: A full day's walk carrying a forty-pound pack and boots.
Day 7: Quiet Day.

In addition to your general training, use the following series of leg and knee exercises to strengthen the ligaments around the knees, the calves and the ankles, all those areas which will endure a great deal of use and punishment on the mountain.

1. Initially step up and step down in rapid succession using a low bench or a step.
2. Hop at speed across a room, forwards and then backwards, alternating to each foot.
3. Using ankle weights raise each foot in turn, first from a lying position, then from a sitting position, finally from a standing position.
4. If your legs become really strong enough, as this is one of the most difficult and strenuous exercises, hop up a flight of stairs on one leg, walk down and then repeat on the other leg. (Those who can and must could try two stairs at a time).

Each of the above exercises to be carried out within a set time for *up to* twenty times each day.

Appendix 6

Necessary Items for the Joint Ascents of Kilimanjaro and Mt Kenya

Clothing	*Equipment*
Boots (well worn-in)	Tent
Trekking Shoes	Large Rucksack
Outer Gloves	Small back-pack
Inner Gloves	Bivouac bag
Stocks (thick and thin)	Sleeping mat
Long underwear	Water bottle, cup and bowl,
Trousers (or ski salopettes)	utensils
Light jacket	Kettle, stove and pot
Windproof over-jacket	Head-torch and hand torch
Over-trousers	First-aid kit
Sweaters	Crampons
Shirts	Ice axes
Hats	Harness (with karabiners)
	Ropes and Prusik loops
	Compass

Bibliography

The Tree Where Man Was Born Peter Matthiessen (William Collins 1972)

Mountains of Kenya Peter Robson (East African Publishing House 1969)

Mountain Walking in Africa David Else (Robertson McCarta Limited 1991)

Backpacker's Africa Hilary Bradt (Bradt Enterprises 1983)

On Top of The World Rebecca Stephens (Macmillan 1994)

Running High Hugh Symonds (Lochar Publishing 1991)

Right Over The Mountain Gill Marais (Element 1991)

When The Iron Eagle Flies Ayya Khema (Penguin Books 1991)

The Zen Way to The Martial Arts Taisen Deshimaru (Penguin Books 1982)

The Elements of Zen David Scott and Tony Doubleday (Element 1992)

Crazy Wisdom Wes Nisker (Ten Speed Press 1990)

Studies in Zen D. T. Suzuki (George Allen & Unwin 1960)